D0984612

THE AUTHOR'S EMPTY PURSE

AND THE RISE OF THE LITERARY AGENT

The Author's Empty Purse
and the Rise of the Literary Agent

by JAMES HEPBURN

London
OXFORD UNIVERSITY PRESS
NEW YORK   TORONTO
1968

Oxford University Press, Ely House, London W.1

GLASGOW NEW YORK TORONTO MELBOURNE WELLINGTON
CAPE TOWN SALISBURY IBADAN NAIROBI LUSAKA ADDIS ABABA
BOMBAY CALCUTTA MADRAS KARACHI LAHORE DACCA
KUALA LUMPUR HONG KONG TOKYO

*Printed in Great Britain
by Ebenezer Baylis and Son, Ltd.
Trinity Press, Worcester, and London*

CONTENTS

ACKNOWLEDGEMENTS

My wife did the research for the first part of Chapter V, and I dedicate the book to her.

I should like to thank Mr. Walter Allen, Mr. Ian Willison of the British Museum, Miss Patricia Butler of A. P. Watt and Son, Mr. Spencer Curtis Brown, Professor Dan H. Laurence, Mr. Peter Lyon, Mr. James Mosley of the St. Bride Foundation Institute Library, Mr. W. H. Ribbans of the National Press Directory, Mr. Wyman W. Parker, the officers of the Society of Authors, Professor Dennis Welland, and Mr. Edgar Wellsman for some very helpful information and assistance.

To the officers of the American Council of Learned Societies I would like to express my gratitude for funds that helped me in preparing the book.

I should like to thank the Oxford University Press for permission to quote from letters by Arnold Bennett and J. B. Pinker (in *Letters of Arnold Bennett*, Vol. 1, Letters to J. B. Pinker); J. M. Dent & Sons and the Trustees of the Joseph Conrad Estate for quotations from Joseph Conrad's letters (in G. Jean-Aubry's *Joseph Conrad: Life and Letters*); Peter Owen Ltd. for part of a letter by Stephen Crane (in Frederick Lewis Allen's *Paul Revere Reynolds*); and the Executors of H. G. Wells for quotations from H. G. Wells's letters (in *The Author*, June and August 1913, and in *The Authors' Handbook for 1935*).

Now Barabbas was a publisher.

(Sometimes attributed to Lord Byron, to whom John Murray sent £1,500 when he heard that Byron was in financial distress.)

Authorship—a vocation which is understood to turn foolish thinking into funds.

(George Eliot, in *Daniel Deronda*, which earned her more than £9,000.)

Mrs. Morland very wittily defined an agent as someone whom you pay to make bad blood between yourself and your publisher.

(Angela Thirkell, in *Pomfret Towers*. Mrs. Thirkell never employed an agent, and left an estate of £74,600.)

I   Introduction: William Heinemann
v. A. P. Watt

> Me, lonely sitting, nor the glimmering light
> Of make-weight candle, nor the joyous talk
> Of loving friend delights; distressed, forlorn,
> Amidst the horrors of the tedious night,
> Darkling I sigh, and feed with dismal thoughts
> My anxious mind, or sometimes mournful verse
> Indite, and sing of groves and myrtle shades,
> Or desp'rate lady near a purling stream,
> Or lover pendant on a willow-tree.
>
> —John Philips, *The Splendid Shilling*, 1705

The rise of the literary agent has been chronicled by only one person, the publisher William Heinemann. His account, which has both charm and accuracy, appeared in the *Athenaeum* in 1893, at a time when the agents had just secured a foothold on literary history:

This is the age of the middleman. He is generally a parasite. He always flourishes. I have been forced to give him some little attention lately in my particular business. In it he calls himself the literary agent. May I explain his evolution?

The Origin. You become the literary agent by hiring an office; capital and special qualifications are unnecessary; but *suaviter in modo* must be your policy, combined with a fair amount of self-assertion. You begin by touting among the most popular authors of the moment, and by being always at hand and glad of a job, you will soon be able to extract from them testimonials which, carefully edited, make up a seductive prospectus to send out broadcast. You must collect these testimonials with zest, just as the pill-doctor or the maker of belts electropathic. It does not much matter how much you pester quiet people for them, as long as you get your circular together. 'You have made one author wealthy (*you*, not his work; oh no, not his work!) who was poor before; another has found you invariably reliable; and a third has tried you two years ago, and has never been anywhere else since.'

The Business. You commence by taking in a weekly paper, in which you follow carefully every author who has hitherto been unsuccessful, who is just beginning to succeed, and who has found a friend in some publisher, whose endeavours and efforts and work have at last helped to bring him into recognition. You must lose no time in dispatching your circular to this author, telling him that he has been shamefully neglected

in the past, that you can double, treble, increase his income tenfold, if
he will only allow you 10 per cent of this income for doing so. . . .

Readers of the time would have recognized in Heinemann's words
a portrait of Alexander Pollock Watt, who was by repute the founder
of the profession of literary agent and who dominated it for a good
many years. In 1893 Watt occupied modest quarters at 2 Paternoster
Square. His investment must indeed have been small, and he pressed
his business to such good advantage that when he died in 1914 he
left behind an estate valued at £60,000. For his training he could
offer more than Heinemann allowed him: thirteen or more years in
association with the publisher Alexander Strahan, notably in the
office of the *Contemporary Review*. And, beginning in 1893, he issued
year by year a volume of testimonial letters from authors whom he
had served well. In 1893 he listed among his clients Grant Allen,
Walter Besant, Wilkie Collins, Arthur Conan Doyle, Rider Haggard,
Thomas Hardy, Bret Harte, and Rudyard Kipling. Their letters
describe the devotion with which Watt pursued their interests. For
Wilkie Collins a business relationship had passed into friendship.
Walter Besant was certain that Watt had tripled his income. There
are even a half-dozen letters from publishers, among them Richard
Bentley and Son and Longmans, Green. Such letters as these last
must have been especially galling to Heinemann. How else could
they have been obtained except by a fair amount of self-assertion?
Only the year before, George Bentley was saying: 'The literary
agency is, I think, a mistake. . . . Nominally the author pays, but
the agent makes us pay.' The fact was that Watt served publishers
as well as authors; and the publisher who yielded to good bargaining
for an author might be the same publisher who welcomed good
bargaining on his own behalf.

Of course the most interesting truth in Heinemann's account—
which apparently followed the first edition of Watt's little book by
a few weeks or months—is that it displays the hostility of publisher
to agent that attended the latter's rise in the world. There were
exceptions—Andrew Chatto, Sr., F. V. White, George Haven
Putnam—but most publishers lamented the intrusion of the middleman into the personal relationship between author and publisher.
They did not mention that they themselves were but recently

middlemen, coming between author and printer-bookseller. And they did not acknowledge that an unpleasantness between themselves and authors was partly responsible for the appearance of the literary agent.

II   The Historical Background:
The Long Quarrel Between Author
and Publisher

WITMORE. What, art thou not cured of scribbling yet?
LUCKLESS. No, scribbling is as impossible to cure as the gout.
WITMORE. And as sure a sign of poverty as the gout of riches.
—Henry Fielding, *The Author's Farce*, 1730

According to Samuel Smiles, it was Thomas Campbell and not Byron who said that Barabbas was a publisher. Whoever it was, by the early nineteenth century the publisher was fit subject for the suspicions of authors, having by then established himself as the dominant figure in the commerce of books. A hundred years before, he was just coming into prominence as an independent figure; and in these and earlier years he had to share his dubious character with the printer, the bookseller, and the patron. The root of the trouble lay in the profession of authorship itself. When Chaucer complained of his empty purse, he exposed the insecurity of a profession that would never be able to guarantee the usefulness, quality, or attractiveness of its wares. Chaucer himself was fortunate in that he could expect patronage from his main profession of public servant; but in another two centuries, when bright young Englishmen were first beginning to regard scribbling as their chief occupation, the situation was commonly disastrous. Witness Thomas Nashe's lament: 'I . . . was despised and neglected, my pains not regarded, or slightly rewarded, and I myself (in prime of my best wit) laid open to poverty. Whereupon (in a malcontent humour) I accused my fortune, railed on my patrons, bit my pen, rent my papers, and raged in all points like a mad man.' Ben Jonson, who was luckier than most of his contemporaries, summed up the general predicament: 'Poetry, in this latter age, hath proved but a mean mistress, to such as have wholly addicted themselves to her.' Though the invention of printing had gradually given commercial value to manuscripts, and the rise in literacy within the sixteenth century itself (from perhaps 30 per cent of the population to 60 per cent) had provided a market,

4

no system had developed whereby the rewards of authorship came as certainly to the author as to others. R. B. McKerrow describes the case of Richard Robinson, who for the pains of authorship might receive from his publisher twenty-six free copies of his book to sell at about a shilling apiece. One of these copies went to the dedicatee, who was expected to be more generous than either the publisher or the public. In one instance the dedicatee gave him £3; in another the dedicatee (this time Queen Elizabeth) gave him nothing. Philip Henslowe's diary mentions numerous young men who earned their literary livelihood so badly that they were frequently in prison and generally in debt. The successful author was the rare one like Shakespeare, who as an actor and full-sharer in the Lord Chamberlain's Company was a kind of publisher of his own work, and who had thereby an independent income.

There were good reasons for the situation developing as badly as it did. In the first place, many authors had not got into the habit of asking for money from printers and booksellers. Sir Philip Sidney was such an author, and his patronage of other authors emphasized his conservative viewpoint. At its best, the attitude was compounded of notions about gentlemanly dignity and the exalted character of art. And for another 300 years it helped to prevent authors from agreeing among themselves to establish principles of payment for their work. Secondly, the ideals of originality and uniqueness in literary work were inadequately developed. Elizabethan authors themselves were appropriating the language and ideas of other writers long after their printers had begun to complain about piracy. And protection came to the printers before it came to the authors. Not until the Copyright Statute of 1709, apparently the first such statute in any country, would it become generally established that an author could hold the copyright to his creation. And for another sixty-five years, the law allowed publishers to buy that right from the author 'for ever', although it had limited copyright to the author for fourteen years, renewable for another fourteen. Both of these reasons for the predicament of the author could be expressed in other more prosaic terms: first, that in the centuries before Elizabeth there had been no occasion and no visible need for authors to develop guilds after the manner of copyists, stationers, bookbinders, and the like; and secondly, that the idea of property was inevitably applied to a physical book long before it was applied to an imaginative act. Thus there was a copyists' guild in 1403, long before any quarrel arose between author and publisher; and by 1557, when the Stationers' Company received its royal charter, the select band of printers and booksellers who largely made up its members constituted a powerful body with clearly defined interests. With negligible exception all copyright was vested in them, and all that an author owned was the physical manuscript that he held in his hand. In order to have it printed, he had no legal choice but to surrender it to a member of the Company—taking it into St. Paul's Churchyard and hawking it among the stationers there.

As H. G. Aldis points out, the situation produced a kind of literary agency. The stationer Thomas Thorpe kept his eye out for likely-looking manuscripts circulating in London. When he came across Shakespeare's sonnets in 1609, he commissioned George Eld to print them, and because he had no shop of his own, he had them sold through two other stationers. He did the same with works by Jonson and Chapman. But the authors were under no obligation to him, nor he to them.

That the condition of the author improved in the course of the next centuries may be ascribed to a variety of causes: rises in population, literacy, leisure, and wealth; the physical and cultural unification of the populace; inevitable refinements in legal doctrine; the increasing dependence of society upon the written word; the accumulating weight of England's literary genius; and the painfully acquired business-sense of her geniuses. In the seventeenth and eighteenth centuries emerged writers such as Milton and Swift whose importance as writers loomed larger than their services to political parties or to the state. In the same centuries Dryden, Pope, and Johnson gained unprecedented national fame largely or wholly on the basis of non-political writing. Dryden earned his living as a writer, and his sense of his importance was great enough to enable him to compose scurrilous verses against his publisher, Jacob Tonson, and to have those verses sent to Tonson with the message: 'Tell the dog that he who wrote these lines can write more.' Alexander Pope was wealthy enough to afford to let publishers bid against one another for his talents. He was possibly the first eminent writer earning his living by his pen who was freely able to do so, and the more than £5,000 he received for his translation of the *Iliad* was one of the consequences. Henry Fielding, who received £1,000 for *Amelia*, said that it was just as dignified for a man to live by writing as by orating. Dr. Johnson could afford to assert that only blockheads did not write for money. And the political hack, Arnall, reportedly earned £10,000 in four years for his services early in the eighteenth century, and retired with a royal pension.

On the other hand, Milton and his widow received a total of £18 for *Paradise Lost*, whose copyright eventually came into the hands of Tonson and helped considerably to fill out his fortune of £80,000. Aphra Behn wrote begging letters to Tonson to ask for £25 instead of £20 for a translation she was doing, and really, she said, she deserved £30. (She seems to have been the first English woman to make a living by writing.) In the Dedication to his *Virgil*, Dryden describes himself as 'worn out with study, and oppressed with fortune'—the result of producing 10,000 lines at 6*d*. a line for Tonson. Pope and Fielding satirized the unscrupulous publishers such as Edmund Curll who lived on the sweat of their hack writers. And in his first ten years in London, Johnson was sometimes in dire poverty. When he was famous, his publishers asked him to name a price for doing the *Lives of the Poets*. He said £200. They finally paid him £300. Later it was admitted that they would have paid £1,000 or more had he demanded it; and their profits were estimated at £5,000 in twenty-five years.

During all these centuries and in fact until nearly the end of the nineteenth century, most reputable writers sold their work outright. The publisher took all the monetary risk, and above his costs he kept all the profit for himself, whether it was meagre or huge. There are cases recorded of virtuous publishers who spontaneously gave additional sums to authors of profitable books; but most such authors had to be content with fame and perhaps a better price on the next book. Few could make a living from their pen, their bargaining position was weak, and they had to be grateful for small favours. Various solutions to the problem were attempted, but none met with anything like general success until the royalty system was introduced. The most thoroughgoing, and for some authors the most alluring, solution was to be one's own publisher; and if one had the wealth of Horace Walpole or professed a high aesthetic line in the manner of William Blake and William Morris, such a solution was feasible and even desirable. For the average author, the experience of George Wither in the 1620s offered the probable result: he confronted a vested interest that was powerful enough to ignore the King himself. In his time Wither was a successful author, and one or another of his works published by ordinary means had considerable circulation. His *Motto*, which he defiantly dedicated 'To Anybody', sold—according to himself—30,000 copies in several editions within a few months. This same work, though, caused one of his three or four imprisonments and in the event reduced him to poverty. When he came out of prison he sought to recoup his fortune by obtaining a patent from James I (apparently through the influence of the Earl of Pembroke) to publish his *Hymnes and Songs of the Church* with sole copyright in his own hands for fifty-one years. Such a patent was the negligible exception to the absolute power of publication held by the Stationers' Company, and it might in this instance have gone uncontested except for the fact that in granting the patent the King additionally stipulated that the *Hymnes* should be included in all bound copies of the Psalms offered for sale by the stationers. Wither borrowed about £300 and had the book printed and distributed, and the Stationers' Company petitioned Wither himself, then the King, and then Parliament to cause the patent to be withdrawn. Failing in these efforts, the Company simply refused to sell the book, and they let it be known that Wither's translations in it were careless, his versification faulty, and his rendering of the Song of Solomon obscene. Wither made legal and literary counter-attacks, notably in *The Schollers Purgatory, Discovered in the Stationers Commonwealth*. This work (published illegally and possibly causing Wither to be imprisoned again) is in part a loquacious defence of Wither's honour as a translator and poet. It also argues the issue of copyright on the grounds of law and equity:

. . . a worshipful lawyer was lately pleased on their [the booksellers'] behalf to say, that the benefit arising from the sale of books was their ancient, and lawful birthright. But if his Mastership's judgment be no better in other cases, I hope to bless myself from his opinions. For unless he can prove, the author hath sold them his birthright (as often he doth, for less than a mess of pottage) he being the elder brother, the right first (by his own law that he professes) falleth unto him. And there are other heirs (but of a collateral line) the printer, and bookbinder that claim just title before the bookseller.

In seeking the patent, Wither says, 'I humbly petitioned the King's most excellent Majesty . . . that according to the laws of nature I might enjoy the benefit of some part of mine own labours.' Furthermore, quite aside from the rights of the matter, the stationers are 'malapert, and arrogant . . . peddlers of books, and for the most part ignorant fellows (acquainted with nothing concerning them, but their names and prices). . . .' The very men who accuse Wither of obscenity publish quantities of scurrilous literature produced by 'hireling authors'. They have become so disreputable that . . .

I wonder so insupportable and so impertinent a thing, as a mere bookseller . . . was ever permitted to grow up in the commonwealth. For, many of our modern booksellers, are but needless excrements, or rather vermin; who being engendered by the sweat of scholars, printers, and bookbinders, do (as worms in timber, or like the generation of vipers) devour those that breed them.

Wither's eloquence availed him nothing but a small immortality. The quarrel lasted eleven years, and he not only lost his investment but during most of that time found himself unable to publish anything through the Stationers' Company itself. In a reply to *The Schollers Purgatory*, published from a manuscript letter in Allan Pritchard's account of the episode (upon which the present discussion largely relies), an associate of the stationers wrote:

The profession of a stationer is to buy and sell, and to gain by it if he can, as all other trades do; they labour to deal in such commodities, as are most vendible; that will turn money readily, whereby they may live. . . . And most of the best authors are not so penurious that they look so much to their gain, as to the good they intend to religion or state. They are too mercenary that write books for money, and their covetousness makes their labours fruitless, and disesteemed.

Until the eighteenth century, the best means by which the author

2

obtained an advantage beyond outright surrender of copyright consisted in payment according to sales. During the time of Elizabeth, impressions of books were for the most part limited to 1,250 and 1,500 copies; and if a book went into a second edition a writer could often obtain an additional sum from his publisher by revising the work. In later years, and still before copyright was ordinarily granted to authors, some authors were in a strong enough position to elicit contracts that stipulated an edition of a certain number, with payment anew to the author upon the printing of each successive edition. *Paradise Lost* was sold under such terms, the publisher, Samuel Simmons, agreeing to pay Milton £5 in advance on each of four editions of 1,300 copies. The first edition sold out in eighteen months, and Milton had his second £5 before he died. The bargain could have been stronger, though. The book sold for 3*s.*, and Simmons was allowed 200 extra copies on each edition on which he paid nothing, so that his net profit must have been well above twenty times what he paid Milton. Of course there was no guarantee that even the first edition would sell out, and George Saintsbury was of the opinion that considering the length, style, and subject, the sale was surprisingly good. Another defender of Simmons thought that the real villain was the largely indifferent public; and he pointed out that even after such a sale, the book was so little valued as a piece of commercial property that Simmons sold the copyright for £25, and it passed from the second publisher to Tonson before it began to yield large profits to anyone. What is immediately significant is that the contract Milton made offered a means by which the author retained some control over his work and some commercial advantage in large sales. As Aldis observes, the system was a forerunner of the royalty system. In France it was used very effectively on the author's behalf, but it never came into widespread use in England.

Three other systems by which the author's interests were to be served were publishing by subscription, commission-publishing, and the half-profit system. Gathering subscriptions guaranteed the market and determined the profit of a book before it was printed, and often before it was written, and the writer could then go to the publisher as employer to employee, offering an attractive agreement for production but reserving the major profit for himself. The method was a common practice in the eighteenth century, and it was in part by this means that Pope made his huge profit on his *Iliad*. Later in the century Cowper subscribed his *Homer*, and obtained £1,000 as against the publisher's fee of £100 and printing costs of £600. Publishing by subscription seems to have been especially useful with the modest publications of scholars as well as with the major works of famous poets; but the general difficulty of writers being their own booksellers must have been all too apparent. In the nineteenth century the subscription clubs, such as the Shakespeare and Camden Societies, appropriated the device, but without aiming to benefit authors. John Petheram (see page 38) had better intentions in 1843, but no one seems to have wanted to join a society whose avowed aim was to help living writers by providing a general subscription of their work. The book clubs of the twentieth century are of course in business for themselves.

Commission publishing was the same method as publishing by subscription, without the subscription. From Elizabethan times onwards, it was mainly the means by which the vanity publisher earned his living. For the fact was that almost no publisher was prepared to be interested in selling a book that offered him no profit beyond his original commission. He fulfilled the letter of the contract—produced a small edition and bound a few copies—and let the book die. The author might assure him that numerous would-be subscribers were waiting to buy the book, but the publisher usually knew better. As late as 1890 the Society of Authors recommended commission-publishing as the best system for the author, but they had to admit that the author needed to be famous or of independent means for it to work. Mark Twain employed it to his own enormous advantage with the sale of *Innocents Abroad*.

The half-profit system worked more to the advantage of both author and publisher; and until the royalty system was introduced, it was fairly often used by reputable writers. Compared with outright sale, it had the characteristic disadvantage of not providing a pre-sale payment to the author; and needy authors could not afford to wait. Then, too, if the book made a loss the author was frequently bound to help sustain it—as John Clare found out when he received a bill for £20 after the publication of his first volume of verse. But if the book sold, the author stood to share profits equally with the publisher. J. W. Croker was reportedly prepared to sell his *Stories from the History of England* to John Murray for £20, but Murray persuaded him to try half-profits, and Croker made £700.[1] What seems to have prevented the half-profit system from becoming the dominant system was (1) the customary absence of advance payment and (2) the apparently often accepted opportunity it gave to publishers to make profits while showing losses. In 1859 James Lowe, the editor of the *Critic*, reported on the subject:

I knew a case in which a charming little book was published by a firm well known in the trade, on the 'half-profit' system; the name of the author was not unknown to the public, and the sale was undoubtedly a very large one; but when the account came to be rendered, *three shillings and sixpence* was the sum tendered to the author as his fair share of the profits. Of course, I don't mean to hint that there had been any foul play here; all that I say is, that the plan is a very bad one. The story is funny enough, and this was not the case of a 'poor author', so that we may fairly laugh at it.

1 Anthony Trollope's account of the sales of his books suggests that he may have lost money by making contracts for outright sale instead of for half-profits. He was one of the few authors of his day who by virtue of regular employment elsewhere and a considerable literary reputation could easily have afforded the delay in payment under half-profits; but he felt that 'a lump sum down was more pleasant than a deferred annuity'. He published his first two novels under half-profits and made nothing; on his third novel he received £20 in advance, with a promise of an additional payment of £30 when 350 copies were sold, and £50 more if 450 copies were sold within six months. The £20 was all he received, and it was in fact his sole literary income during his first twelve years of writing. He then sold *The Warden* on half-profits and made about £20 in two years on it, with sales totalling a few hundred copies. (In all, about 700 copies seem to have been sold in the first five or six years.) *Barchester Towers* followed, likewise under half-profits, though Trollope obtained £100 in advance on it. Sales likewise were small. Thereafter he insisted on outright sale, and took his next novel, *The Three Clerks*, from Longmans to Bentley because Longmans would not publish it except under half-profits. Bentley gave him £250, and then Chapman and Hall gave him £400 for *Dr. Thorne*. Presently, between serial publication and book publication, Trollope was obtaining as much as £3,000 outright per novel. The point is, though, that as he established his reputation over the years, *The Warden* and *Barchester Towers* continued to sell, and by 1876 they had earned him £727. 11s. 3d., or more than he obtained outright for the sale of *The Three Clerks* and *Dr. Thorne*. Writing in 1876, Trollope asserted that *Dr. Thorne* was the best seller of all his novels. Presumably he would have done better with it under half-profits, just as he eventually earned more with *The Warden* and *Barchester Towers* than the £100 or £200 that he might have obtained for each of them in the mid-fifties had he sold them outright.

He also recalled another case in which the author's profits were to begin after a certain number of copies were sold. Astonishingly enough, the sales began to fade away as the magic number came in sight, and they finally stopped altogether within seven of it. After some months of this, the author secretly bought seven copies himself, but the next account showed no change. He took the matter to court, and won his case; but according to Lowe, the talk along Paternoster Row was that the publisher had made a mistake in arithmetic.

Eight years later, James Spedding, a writer and a friend of Tennyson and Fitzgerald, printed at his own expense two essays under the title of *Publishers and Authors*. In a prefatory note he explains that the essays were rejected by magazine editors not because they were uninteresting or unfair or ineffectual but because they would offend publishers and thereby damage the magazine that printed them. The offence mainly concerns Spedding's analysis of the half-profit system. He acknowledges at the outset that he does not know in detail how the half-profit system works and that no one else apart from the publishers seems to know either. Publishers simply do not divulge their accounts, or if they do divulge them they do not explain them, or if they do explain them they do not show vouchers for expenses, or if they are brought into court and forced to divulge, explain, and show, there are often discrepancies, costs where there have not been costs, and profits before profits. What seems to be the case even when the publisher is reputable is that every item of publishing expense bears a hidden surcharge, so that the publisher does have earnings before profits officially begin. The amount of surcharge varies, and can be increased with impunity. Publishers justify the surcharge by saying that of course they must be repaid for their time, trouble, and skill in dealing with stationer, printer, binder, and others; but they rarely if ever mention the surcharge in negotiating with authors and they rarely if ever define the charge. Thus the author hardly ever knows what he is bargaining for, and assuredly he is not bargaining for half the profit. An author might expect, for instance, on a book whose publishing costs might reasonably be supposed to be about £600 and which would probably sell out an edition of 1,000 copies at 36s., that he would share half a total profit of £1,200. But Spedding knows of such an instance where the author's share proved to be £50, the 'costs' ultimately consuming £1,700 of the £1,800 gross receipts. Possibly, says Spedding, the particular publisher could not have undertaken the task without the surcharges. Very well. But does not the author have an equal right to know beforehand the likely reward for his labour, so that he may also decide not to undertake the task?

The problem is susceptible of easy solution, says Spedding. In New York, he has been informed, the Hurd and Houghton company uses a new system, called the royalty system, to pay its authors. With this method, the publisher estimates his costs and, if he wants, adds a surcharge; he estimates probable sales at a given retail price; he estimates what further profit he wants to make. Then, without divulging any of this, he tells the author that, say, a royalty of 2.8 per cent on an edition of 1,000 copies selling at 36s. is what he can afford to offer. The author is thus able to know what his probable reward is and whether to enter into the bargain. He may try to see how much royalty another publisher would offer. In the course of time, reasonable royalties for particular sorts of books would become generally established, and the publisher who was out to make unwarranted profits at the expense of his authors would be a marked man. It is true that any publisher could still cheat by under-reporting sales; but this would be clearly cheating, whereas the surcharges under the half-profit system cannot so readily be adjudged dishonest. The surcharges leave authors with grounds for suspicion at every point in the proceedings.

How much influence Spedding's little book had is unknown, but how great an improvement the royalty system represented over the half-profit system and also over outright sale is attested by the fact that during the next thirty years the royalty system swept away the other two. Its rise coincided with the rise to power of the literary agent, and the two of them together set the seal upon the improved bargaining position of authors.

The most solid evidence of the author's improved situation over the centuries was the increase in price he won for his wares, culminating in the £20,000 that Macaulay received in one celebrated cheque for his *History*. In this respect the publisher was sometimes the hero of the piece, and any tale of the hardships of authors needs to be interleaved with remarks about honest, generous, and far-sighted publishers. Robert Dodsley was one, himself an author as well as a publisher, and he and others earned Dr. Johnson's praise of the booksellers as the real patrons of literature: 'I respect Andrew Millar, sir, he raised the price of literature.' When John Murray heard that Byron was in financial straits he sent him £1,500 and promised another such sum should Byron need it. Byron, whose birthright and eminence made him one of the few poets able to treat publishers as tradesmen, replied that Murray's action 'sets my opinion of you, and indeed of human nature, in a different light from that in which I have been accustomed to consider it'. But another of Murray's authors, and a personal friend, Isaac D'Israeli, had already established the dominant public tone for author-publisher relations in the nineteenth century. In the same year that Byron awoke to find himself famous, D'Israeli published his classic *Calamities of Authors*. 'What affectionate parent', says D'Israeli, 'would consent to see his son devote himself to his pen as a profession? . . . Most authors close their lives in apathy or despair, and too many live by means which few of them would not blush to describe.' His book is a compendium of calamities, not least of which is the mere fact of having to write for money. And when D'Israeli reconciles himself to that fact, he is confronted with another: 'Authors continue poor, and booksellers become opulent, an extraordinary result!' He did not foresee that later he would write an essay on 'authors who have ruined their publishers' or that his own son would happily obtain £10,000 from a publisher for *Endymion*, a sum that the publisher seems not to have recouped. The record of the nineteenth century is the continuing improvement of the condition of the author and the continuing outcry of calamity.

The century saw a rapid development in some of the conditions of improvement. In one or another account they are described as a grand forward march of culture, social democracy, technology, population, and law. As hard facts they were the advance in new book production from about 370 titles in 1800 to about 6,000 in 1900; the virtual wiping out of illiteracy through working-men's classes, the Free Library Act of the mid-century, and the Education Act of 1870; the physical capacity to produce 5,000 copies of a newspaper a day in 1800 as against a million in 1900; the increase in population from around ten million to almost forty million; copyright legislation at home in 1842 to protect native writers and publishers from pirates across the borders, and copyright legislation in America in 1891 that began to protect British writers against piracy there. R. K. Webb observes that all this progress was probably accompanied by a decline in the reading habit; but the total volume of reading or turning of pages vastly increased, as one more statistic suggests: a rise in the domestic production of paper from 11,000 tons in 1800 to more than 650,000 tons in 1900. The advance was of particular significance in the expansion of periodical literature, for it was here that the ordinary skilled writer—as against Pope or Byron—was able in increasing numbers to earn a living wage. Again the statistical evidence is impressive: some 250 newspapers in the United Kingdom in 1800 and 2,500 in 1900, including an increase in daily newspapers from perhaps half a dozen to 240 or more; a rise in the circulation of *The Times* from less than 5,000 to around 60,000, and of the cheaper dailies from perhaps 2,500 to the *Daily Mail*'s 500,000. In 1818 the *Edinburgh Review* and the *Quarterly Review* had impressive sales of 14,000 each; but the flood of magazines that later usurped their power often had much higher figures: the *Cornhill* began with 110,000 in 1860, and more popular journals such as *Household Words* and *All the Year Round* began above 100,000 and the latter rose to 300,000 in 1869. These figures themselves were dwarfed by those of the very cheap magazines that came into prominence in the last quarter of the century: *Lloyd's Weekly Newspaper*, *Tit-Bits*, *Answers*, and *Pearson's Weekly* all rising above half a million at one time or another, and *Harmsworth's Magazine* and the *Royal Magazine* going to around a million at the turn of the century.

Just as such figures ignore the number of people who gave up reading *Pilgrim's Progress* and the Bible every day, so they ignore the numberless chapbooks, broadsides, tracts, and unstamped newssheets that provided much of the popular reading fare at the beginning of the century and earlier, and that diminished in importance later. In the 1820s and 1830s James Catnach sold accounts of notorious murders that ranged into millions of copies; and religious societies countered his activities by giving away tens of thousands of tracts at public executions. But such literature itself argues the improving condition of the writer; for what the writer needed was the more regular paid employment that the later cheap press and the more respectable press began to provide.[1]

The earnings of most writers in the nineteenth century were not enviable, but the writers saw so many markets burgeoning about them that they had reason for hope. An article in *Fraser's Magazine* in 1847 describes the middle region of Grub Street, with some glimpses of the lower end and the upper reaches. Only one book in thirty brings any money at all to the author; on the rest he either makes nothing or loses. Poems, sermons, morals, and metaphysics rarely command a price. History pays. Novels by popular authors command £100 to £500, and occasionally £1,500 if the name is Edward Bulwer. Novels by writers who have reputations in other fields are published on the half-profit system. First novels are never paid for. Novels by ladies and gentlemen cost their muses £50 to £200. The situation is better with periodical literature; and anyone who complains that magazines and newspapers are the plague of the age should be made aware of the fact that it is only through them that most professional authors are able to survive. An author who could not obtain sixpence for a book on Chinese antiquities can write articles on them and find a well-paying market. The best quarterlies often pay £50 to £100 for such articles, and the ordinary contributor to them can earn £16 to £20 a sheet. Writers who have talent for journalism can easily earn 15s. a column for their work. In sum, the article says, literature is at last almost as stable a means of earning a living as the Bar or the Church. Fortunately it is not very lucrative, for it might become debased; but on the average a man can earn £300 a year by it, enough to live like a gentleman (while not writing like one).

---

1 Most of the figures in these two paragraphs have been drawn from the following sources (their roundness is meant to indicate imprecision): R. D. Altick, *The English Common Reader*; the *Author*; the *Cambridge History of English Literature*, Vol. 14; the *Guide to English Literature*, ed. Boris Ford, Vols. 5 and 6; the *Literary Year-Book*; Marjorie Plant, *The English Book Trade*; the *Publishers' Circular*.

Some of the figures reported in the article may not be entirely reliable, but only the last is unlikely. It probably reflects the earnings of some of the more successful writers. George Henry Lewes, who was an unusually clever and prolific essayist, averaged slightly under £400 a year for the years 1842 to 1861. Only for a brief period, 1862 to 1866, did he earn much more, and then his income ranged between £600 and £1,300 a year. One of the other figures is particularly interesting in that it suggests how far the ordinary successful writer had come in forty-five years. In 1802 when the *Edinburgh Review* began, the proprietors made an unprecedented decision to pay their contributors a high price for their articles. It was thought that some might regard it as undignified to accept an honorarium, but whatever feelings did arise, the proffered payment of £10 a sheet was accepted. The editor of the *Review* was himself to receive £200 a year; and the first editor to be offered the sum, Francis Jeffrey, wrestled with his conscience and decided that he too could accept 'without being supposed to have suffered any degradation'. Anyone who thinks of John Keats 'leaving great verse unto a little clan' may imagine that the money-minded men of the *Edinburgh Review* and its rival *Quarterly* (1809) were fit creatures to disparage his work: already debased practitioners of a lucrative profession, and men whom the literary agent would further debase. That is a viewpoint that came to full flower in another fifty years.

What of the lower end of Grub Street? There swarmed the thousands to whom £50 for an article was an idle dream. Till the end of the century they laboured for half a crown for anonymous paragraphs in cheap magazines, a guinea for a short story. But even the cheapest magazine sometimes fulfilled dreams. *Tit-Bits*, which began in 1881 and was selling 200,000 copies after two years, ran a multitude of contests by which aspiring writers might compete for five, ten, and twenty-five guineas. On one notable occasion they offered a prize of £1,000 for the best light serial story. The consequence was unexpected, appalling, and overwhelming. More than twenty thousand manuscripts came in—proof if ever there was proof of the literary longings nurtured by the amelioration of literary calamity. When the editors offered another twenty guineas for a parody of the prize-winning entry, Grant Allen's *What's Bred in the*

Bone, the new sum provided the first known literary earnings of Arnold Bennett.[1]

The lower end of Grub Street was, in fact, not so terrifying as formerly, and it does not need a perverse fancy to see this in George Gissing's novel. The moral of his tale is that virtue is unrewarded in this world, an unexceptionable moral that he has the artistic licence to illustrate with the poverty and death of the serious writers Reardon and Biffen, and the success of the facile Milvain. In the last chapter, 'Rewards', when Whelpdale is shedding a tear for Reardon and Biffen, Milvain says to him: 'My dear fellow, compose yourself and be logical . . . ; success has nothing whatever to do with moral deserts.' So composed, one looks at the novel not as a work of art but as a picture of life and of the commercial prospects of literature in the 1880s. Biffen's suicide, it is plain, has nothing directly to do with commercial failure: it stems from a hopeless and foolish passion for Amy Reardon. True that he might not have the passion if his poverty did not prohibit marriage; but true also that prior to his passion he ekes out a livelihood by miscellaneous work, takes much pleasure in life, writes an honest novel that his friends—serious and facile alike—agree is utterly dull, and finds a publisher for it. His art is realistic, his life unrealistic except that he knows his expectations. What improvement in the condition of writers would ever save such an uncompromising, unpromising, and foolish person?

Reardon is a better writer than Biffen, has a deserved success in selling one of his novels for £100, and allows his energies to be dissipated in trying to support himself and Amy beyond their means. Not so unbending as Biffen, he produces a potboiler; but more absurdly, he tries to prevent Milvain from writing a favourable review of it. He gives up writing after returning to the very conditions under which he wrote successfully. He yields his career and

---

1 In 1966 in the *Guardian* David McKie reported on a competition run by Peter Owen and Mayflower Books to find a new writer. The prize or prizes totalled £1,000, and more than a thousand manuscripts came in, none of them apparently of much worth. Mr. McKie surmised that 'the sad thing about the present situation is that this great army of unpublished writers seems likely to keep growing'. Doubtless he was right, if only in view of the increasing population of the world. But the experience of the editors of *Tit-Bits* suggests that the real heyday of literary aspiration was the late nineteenth century, when literature was more likely to be the first thought of anyone with an urge to create.

his life without a struggle. 'I suppose', he says, 'there must be some rich man somewhere who has read one or two of my books with a certain interest. If only I could encounter him and tell him plainly what a cursed state I am in, perhaps he would help me to some means of earning a couple of pounds a week. One has heard of such things.' Amy replies: 'In the old days.' She might have added: In the new days there are literary agents. Curiously enough, at about the same time that Gissing wrote the novel, Edmund Gosse gave a talk in which he asserted that in one respect the Grub Street of the 1880s was worse than that of the 1740s: the hapless author in those earlier days might find a patron. Gosse himself was old-fashioned, and could not countenance the literary agent.

The novel does show a variety of ways by which people of modest gifts and some determination can earn a living from literature. Milvain's sisters are casually urged by him to write, and because he has an eye for the market, he knows how they can earn £30 readily enough. It is a sum that would enable Biffen to live for almost a year under his spartan regime. Marian Yule is assured by Milvain that if she wants she can earn £100 to £150 a year at light fiction, enough to support herself very respectably. Hinks, who is married, makes £100 a year at nameless work, and is able to spend £30 of it on books. The uninspired Alfred Yule makes £250 a year at criticism and scholarship. Biffen's friend Sykes supports his inclination for drink by writing autobiographies and illustrated histories of the United States. He reads Biffen a lecture on the literary market: never write realism for the lower classes; they want romance in their lives. And Jasper Milvain himself? As the novel opens he has earned £35 in the first three quarters of the year (1882). The previous year he earned £25. Neither sum provides the bare subsistence that a man such as he needs, and he has no hesitation in obtaining money from his family, for he infallibly knows that by meeting the right people and playing the right market he will have £1,000 a year in ten years. (It took Edmund Gosse eleven years, from 1874 to 1885, to rise from £112 to £970 a year.) He realizes that his talents are ordinary, and he declares that 'the end of literary work—unless one is a man of genius—is to secure comfort and repute'. Within a year he can describe a day of triumph to his sisters. At breakfast at seven-thirty he began to read a book for review, and by ten-thirty the review was done. From eleven to one he wrote his weekly causerie. From two to five he wrote half of one essay, and from seven to nine part of another. What is the worth of it all? asks sister Maud. Ten to twelve guineas, he replies. And the literary worth? 'Equal to that of the contents of a mouldy nut', he says.

So one is brought back to the more sympathetic and more genuinely gifted Reardon. Passive and unrealistic as he is, could he not survive? The answer is an unequivocal yes. Milvain estimates that on a novel on which Reardon made £100 or less, he might have made £400 or more. It would have meant dickering with magazine and newspaper editors on serial rights, second serial rights, foreign publication—all sorts of things. This is no longer Johnson's Grub Street, says Milvain, but a great international world 'supplied with telegraphic communication'. What neither Milvain nor Gissing adds is that Reardon would not have had to do the dickering himself. The literary agent was on the scene, specially equipped to handle the increasingly complex and mysterious business end of literature, and he presently began to help both passive and energetic literary types. There is, of course, a literary agent in the novel—Whelpdale, the failed novelist, the hapless lover, the man who casts about for any way to survive. Whelpdale could not have helped Reardon; but a more capable man might have. Gissing should have sent Reardon to A. P. Watt—just as he advised his own brother to go to Watt, some little while before writing *New Grub Street*.

III Precursors of the True Agents: Vanity Publishers, Critics, Friends, and Others

An author is really a whimsical creature! There is such a pride, and self-conceit, mixed with the most hungry necessity.

—Anonymous, *The Author's Triumph*, 1737

A good many years before Edwin Reardon's death, the young Pendennis was taken down to Grub Street by his friend Warrington, was initiated into that arcane world, and eventually made a success. Lucky the young man willing to be helped; lucky the young man with such a friend. Warrington was in fact a literary agent before the time of literary agents, and he performed a task that others had been doing as long as authors have had friends. To find the original agent among these friends is impossible, and all one can do is to trace the variety of precursors who gradually transformed themselves into true agents, charging 10 per cent for their friendship. For the sake of irony the story must begin with the publishers themselves, who in their activity of vanity publication had been the friends of authors for a long time. Even in Elizabethan days, when gentlemen professed not to think it proper to have their poems printed, many paid for the pleasure; and when publishing became respectable, and to be a gentleman still presupposed a talent for versifying, the vanity press remained at hand to help him as well as maiden ladies and other literary aspirants. One thing that particularly made the vanity publisher a forerunner of the literary agent was his willingness to advertise himself as the friend of authors known and unknown. The middle of the nineteenth century seems to have been especially rich in the agency of vanity publication, with such advertisements as *The Author's Hand-Book* (1844), *The Search for a Publisher* (1855), and *How to Publish* (1857) paving the way to the vanity publisher's door. These were writers' manuals; and the second one, which went through eight editions, is a fine example of the type. It begins with a description of the publisher as a figure especially created to be the author's agent in his dealings with the printer and the public. Has the author heard terrible stories of the rapacity of publishers? Believe none of them! The real interest of the publisher cannot fail to be the real interest of the author; and all the trivial and onerous burdens of publication—so wearisome to an author that were he himself to undertake them he might die and his manuscript be lost—can be profitably transferred to the broad shoulders of the trained publisher. There follows a description of typical contractual arrangements between author and publisher. The publisher of the manual (whose name happens to be Cash) prefers the commission system, whereby the author reaps greater profit when the book begins to sell. In the manner of A. P. Watt's little book, the manual offers testimonial letters from contented authors, from William Rands, author of *The Frost Upon the Pane*, from Louisa Costello, author of *Anne of Brittany*, and from others. All the letters are dated May 1855.

Needless to say, writers ought to be protected from such friends. But perhaps not too carefully. *The Search for a Publisher* was issued for twenty-six years by a series of obscure publishers at several different addresses, and the contented authors remained the same through five editions and disappeared thereafter. What is more to the point is that the vanity publisher must have seemed to many an untried author to be the only sympathetic intermediary between him and the public until the literary agent came along. And the manuals of the vanity publishers seem to have been among the first of the self-help manuals on writing.[1] Such manuals flourished

---

[1] The two earliest manuals I saw were both prepared by the printer Caleb Stower. The material for authors in them became a customary part of later self-help manuals. The first, *Typographical Marks Employed in Correcting Proofs, Explained and Exemplified; For the Use of Authors*, London, 1806 (2nd edition), consists of a few pages explaining and illustrating the use of correction symbols. By way of preface Stower says:

An imperfect description of the *marks* employed in correcting proofs was published many years ago, in a work [*The Printer's Grammar*] exclusively confined to printers, and which has been long out of print; it was therefore thought that a more public account of them would tend to save time and expense, and would not be altogether unacceptable to authors and booksellers. Errors are frequently committed by the printer, from the obscure manner in which authors make their corrections and alterations; it is therefore desirable that the common mode, with which all printers are well acquainted, should be clearly understood and adopted by every author.

The other book, *The Printer's Price-Book*, London, 1814, is mainly directed to fellow printers, and consists largely of specimen pages of various kinds of type and setting; but a few pages are addressed to authors with regard to typographical marks.

[*cont.*]

towards the end of the century along with the agents. In 1882 Wyman and Sons published a guide for authors on the mechanical aspects of publication: kinds of paper, type, illustrations, contracts. Much of its detail would have been found in the partial accounts of the vanity publishers. In 1886 Percy Russell published a *Literary Manual*, which sprinkled information about the yearly sales of popular authors on to a general account of the forms of writing. This book was imitated and improved upon many times, notably by Arnold Bennett's *How to Become an Author* of 1903.

The vanity publisher did not make a good agent, and it was in the office of the reputable publisher that some of the more helpful precursors of the literary agent were to be found. Of course there is the sense—slightly distorted in *The Search for a Publisher*—in which all publishers were agents of authors. They shared this honour with patrons, printers, and booksellers, with anyone who helped to bring a manuscript before the public. The ideal figure was such a publisher as John Taylor, who served John Keats so well, or F. S. Ellis, who was first a bookseller friend of D. G. Rossetti's and then his publisher. (Reportedly Smith, Elder paid Rossetti £9 for *Early Italian Poets* in 1861, and friend Ellis paid him £450 for the *Poems* of 1870.) In this light the publishers were an evolutionary phenomenon in a progressive division of commercial labour, and the literary agents were the inevitable next phenomenon, hard on their heels, taking away some of the publishers' function just as the publishers took away some of the booksellers' and patrons'. When Dr. Johnson called the bookseller-publishers 'the patrons of literature' he was regarding the matter in such a light. And the continuing truth of it can be seen today in the fact that literary agents to a considerable extent perform

---

This book is especially interesting in the light of the later quarrel between publishers and the Society of Authors with regard to the costs of publishing (see below, pp. 77–8). Of the Society's book, *The Cost of Publishing*, one or more publishers asserted that the figures were meaningless, since it was impossible to generalize about costs. The Society responded by suspecting that the publishers did indeed have something to hide. Stower anticipates this quarrel in his prefatory remarks. He offers the book as a guide to the inexperienced printer, and says that the sums he lists are regular trade charges, which will vary under special conditions. 'Some might object', he says, 'to the giving publicity to these charges; but to me and to many of my experienced friends in the trade, there appear no grounds for such objection.' Stower describes himself here as editor of *The Printer's Grammar*, which was issued in 1787 and which contained no advice to authors.

the service of first reader to the publishers. (A more detailed evolutionary chart would put the publisher's reader himself, and allied
figures, in between the publisher and the agent. The systematically
employed reader seems to have arrived by the beginning of the
nineteenth century—though to this day the employment of individual readers is often casual and brief.) At any rate, the friend of
authors was often the friend of publishers. He might be a publisher
himself, an editor, a reader, an accountant, or a respected acquaintance. His history traces back to the patronage that Sir Philip
Sidney bestowed upon other writers and to the assistance that
Gabriel Harvey, Thomas Nashe, and others probably gave to the
stationer John Wolfe in finding other literary hacks to serve him.

The nineteenth century abounded in examples of such informal
literary agency, the most intimate being the services that Henry
Austen performed for his sister, that George Henry Lewes performed for George Eliot, and that the three Trollopes performed for
one another. Among the celebrated instances was that of George
Meredith, who obtained a publisher for his first book of poems
with the assistance of his father-in-law, Thomas Love Peacock, who
was a friend of the publisher. When Meredith later became a reader
for Chapman and Hall, he went out of his way to offer advice to
writers; and he was remembered by Hardy and Gissing as having
particularly encouraged their ambitions. Chapman and Hall were
ready to publish Hardy's first novel if Hardy contributed a sum of
money by way of subsidy; but Meredith recommended that Hardy
not publish it but instead write another novel along different lines.
Hardy took the advice, and *Desperate Remedies* was the result. A
more substantial intermediary between author and publisher was
the Scottish literary critic, George Gilfillan, who at mid-century
spoke with a voice almost as powerful as Carlyle's. In an account
of him, W. Robertson Nicoll remarked that 'almost every literary
aspirant in the country sent his manuscripts to the Dundee critic. ...
Generous and warmhearted to a degree, Gilfillan took endless
troubles for his young admirers. He criticized; he praised where he
could; he found publishers in many cases.' Among other writers, he
discovered Sydney Dobell and Alexander Smith. In 1869 the *Publishers' Circular* remarked caustically on two publishing houses that

had accepted manuscripts on the advice of a 'pseudo-critic' and a newspaper writer. And towards the end of the century Andrew Lang wrote a sardonic article on the numberless amateur writers who sent him and others their unsolicited manuscripts, asking for advice. Lang was certain that people who were so presumptuous must lack the sensitivity to be good writers. He had no intention of turning himself into a despised agent. But Gilfillan and many others in a similar situation were more sympathetic.

Two of the most notable informal agents in the whole century were John Forster and T. Watts-Dunton. The latter is the less interesting in that he served Swinburne at a time when the professional agent was on the scene; but he possessed qualities frequently found in the true agents: a legal background and a worshipful attitude towards literature. From about 1880 onwards he supervised Swinburne's literary affairs, finding publishers for his articles, negotiating the proposed transfer of Swinburne's affiliation from Chatto and Windus to Chapman and Hall, and restraining Swinburne's muse. Doubtless he was the least appealing of the informal agents. John Forster was another sort of man, who had a distinguished literary career of his own and was an equal among the writers whom he helped. Arthur Waugh said of him that 'he bridged the gulf between the patron of the eighteenth century and the literary agent of the twentieth'; and Thackeray said: 'Whenever anybody is in a scrape we all fly to him for refuge—he is omniscient and works miracles.' Tennyson, Landor, Carlyle, and Dickens were among those who sought refuge. When he first met Dickens in 1836, Forster was trying to find a publisher for Browning's *Sordello* and a stage for *Strafford*. Within a year, he and Dickens were firm friends, and the friendship proved to be the most enduring and intimate in Dickens's life. From then on, Forster saw and commented on most of Dickens's work in manuscript, and he also assumed the task of proof-reading. He did most of the negotiating with John Macrone, publisher of *Sketches by Boz*, in the attempt to prevent Macrone from reissuing the book. For more than two years he was involved in the quarrel with Richard Bentley over Dickens's editorship of *Bentley's Miscellany* and the contract with Bentley for two novels. Bentley had every legal right on his side, and he yielded repeatedly to Dickens's demands for higher salary, increased payments for the novels, and the like, only to find each time that his satisfied author was no longer satisfied. All that Dickens had on his side was the knowledge that day by day he was becoming a more valuable piece of literary property to Bentley, in part because Chapman and Hall's instalments of *Pickwick Papers* were making a sensation. Signed contracts took no notice of the fact. As Edgar Johnson put it, Dickens had no case, but he had a grievance. It was the quarrel between author and publisher in ideal form. John Forster shared the argument equally with Dickens and Dickens's solicitor. Subsequently he was principal negotiator in some of Dickens's dealings with Chapman and Hall, and with the printers Bradbury and Evans, who handled *Household Words*. During Dickens's second American trip he held power of attorney. He also advised Dickens on non-literary matters, notably the break-up of Dickens's marriage. In this last capacity he was equally fulfilling the activities of literary agents after him.

Forster's work for Dickens was unpaid. So was Watts-Dunton's for Swinburne. Meredith was paid by Chapman and Hall, not by Hardy. The literary patron did the paying himself. To find an agent paid by the author among the predecessors of the true agents, one must turn to the vanity publisher, to Dickens's solicitor, to an author's accountant, or to any other person hired by an author to help him handle his literary affairs. There were many such figures in the nineteenth century, connected with other arts as well as with literature. Of them all, the theatrical agents most obviously resemble the true literary agents. One of the earliest of these was John Lee (1795-1881). He trained as an actor, and appeared as Laertes in a famous production of *Hamlet* at Drury Lane in 1828. His great success was as Jingle in an unauthorized stage version of *Pickwick Papers* in 1837. From 1826 to 1833 he was Edmund Kean's secretary-agent, taking over from a man named Phillips, who seems to have been with Kean as early as 1815. He made arrangements with managers, communicated with the press, and accompanied Kean on tour. 'What day do I open in Cheltenham?' Kean wrote to him in 1831. He was well paid for his work and was one of Kean's intimate friends. In the forties, some years after Kean's death, Lee set himself up as a theatrical agent in Bow Street, Covent Garden, presumably offering his services to all comers. The large number of touring actors and touring companies during the century offered rich opportunities for such agents, and it is curious that they seem to have had little or no direct effect upon the rise of literary agency— though there is no doubt that some of the dramatic work carried on by literary agents derives directly from theatrical agency. A companion-figure who came into prominence after the middle of the century was the lecture agent, whose most famous clients were usually literary men. George Dolby (d. 1900), who was connected with the operatic and entertainment stage most of his life, managed Charles Dickens's readings from 1866 to 1870, and reportedly made £3,000 doing so. The most famous lecture agent in America was a Scotsman, James Redpath (1833–91). He went to America when he was fifteen and became a well-known newspaperman and then an unsuccessful publisher. In 1867 or 1868 he was co-founder of the Boston Lyceum Bureau, which arranged lectures and lecture tours. Until his time, lecture committees in America apparently applied directly to a lecturer or reader, and offered fees from $50 to $100. Redpath was usually his own lecture committee, and he paid fees up to $1,000 out of the sale of tickets. In some instances he seems to have paid flat fees, and reaped whatever additional profit there was; in others he seems to have charged a 10 per cent fee, in the manner of literary agents after him. Associated with him for a time was James Burton Pond (Major Pond; 1838–1903), who had a brief career as an informal literary agent. Pond spent his early years as a printer, editor, and newspaperman. In 1873 he was working on the *Salt Lake Tribune* in Utah, and became interested in helping the estranged wife of Brigham Young, the Mormon leader. He did some of the writing of her book, *Wife No. 19*, found a publisher for it, and then became her lecture agent. Along with Redpath, and later as an independent agent, he managed lectures and tours for Mark Twain, Walt Whitman, William Dean Howells, and many English writers, including Dickens, Matthew Arnold, Hall Caine, Conan Doyle, and Anthony Hope. Doubtless the rewarding service of the lecture agent impressed writers, especially when international doors were thereby opened. It is sometimes said that literary agency arose mainly as a consequence of the possibility of international copyright; and though this is not true, the spur to literary agency that came in the nineties owed much to the fact of international copyright legislation at that time; and the international literary agents did something of the same job as the international lecture agents before them.

One other international figure of the time is worth mentioning, Henry Stevens (1819–86)—Henry Stevens of Vermont, as he was pleased to say. Most of his career was devoted to dealing in rare books: plundering England for private and public collectors in America, and plundering America for the British Museum, whose agent he was from 1846 onwards. His fee was a 10 per cent charge above the price of the books he purchased. He also found time for other literary activity. In the fifties he became an agent for one or two of the American publishers who respected English copyright, buying English copies of works for sale in America. He forwarded books from Thomas Carlyle to Ralph Waldo Emerson, thereby assisting in the informal literary agency that the two writers performed for each other in obtaining 'authorized' publications of their works in America and England. In addition he was an agent for English periodicals in the effort to defeat piracy of them in America. He copyrighted the articles in America, and imported copies to sell to libraries and private persons. During the Civil War, when his career as a bookman was deteriorating, he was a Union agent for the purchase of arms in England. In the late seventies, when his situation was still worse, he was listed in the London *Post Office Directory* as a 'literary agent', though whether he was an agent in any other sense than he had been before is not known. His biographer, Wyman W. Parker, is unaware that he ever did anything more than forward manuscripts of friends to likely publishers.

Such paid agents were largely a consequence of the growing complexity of literary and artistic activity, both nationally and internationally. It is hardly surprising, then, that the first great businessman of letters, Sir Walter Scott, employed paid agents. According to H. J. C. Grierson, Scott was very conscious of his commercial worth, and was determined that he himself instead of a publisher should extract the main profit. That he brought ruin to himself and helped to ruin Archibald Constable, who was a generous publisher, suggests that he should have employed better agents than the Ballantyne brothers. Part of Scott's method was to become a secret partner in the printing firm of James Ballantyne and Company in 1805 or 1806, and his contracts with Constable and other publishers called for printing with Ballantyne. He was also a founding and secret partner in the publishing firm of John Ballantyne, which came into existence in 1809, when Scott had a short-lived quarrel with Constable. Between them, the Ballantyne brothers published several of Scott's works and printed all of them. Both firms ran into financial difficulties, in part because of Scott's personal extravagance and his enthusiasm for unprofitable publishing ventures. John Ballantyne's firm went into liquidation in 1813; and from 1816 until 1822 Scott was sole head of the printing firm, employing James Ballantyne as his manager at a salary of £400. Especially after 1813, the brothers handled Scott's dealings with publishers. Scott seems always to have made the decisions, but the brothers approached the publishers, suggested terms, played off John Murray against Constable, and concluded agreements. Grierson says that they were 'absolutely at Scott's beck and call'. Most of the work fell to John. In addition he was frequently Scott's amanuensis, while James was literary adviser, correcting Scott's style and punctuation. In 1821 John died, and in 1826 came the great crash of the Constable, Scott, and Ballantyne fortunes, and the law stepped in to provide Scott with another literary agent. The Bank of Scotland was part-agent, but the active member was Scott's own law agent, John Gibson, who thenceforward conducted and controlled negotiations for Scott's work. He bargained with a London publisher for the novel *Woodstock*, decided that the publisher was unreliable, and bargained again with Longmans. He concluded a generous agreement, wrote to Scott about it, and received from Scott such a letter as any grateful author might write to his protector: 'My dear Sir—You have made a glorious sale. Tom Campbell at a literary dinner gave Bonaparte for his toast, alleging for a reason that he had once hanged a bookseller. You have overshot one in his own bow.' (The unlucky man was Johann Phillip Palm of Nuremberg, who was shot in 1806 for publishing a pamphlet against the rule of the French in Germany.)

It is unlikely that many prominent or prolific authors after Scott's time did not make some use of a personal agent, paid or unpaid. One later paid agent, worth mentioning because he served at least two writers, was Moncure D. Conway (1832–1907). He was born in Virginia, went to Harvard Divinity School, and became a Unitarian minister. In 1863 he came to England, and from then until 1884 he was minister at South Place Chapel in London. He also served on the staffs of the *Daily News* and the *Pall Mall Gazette*. He knew many of the most famous American and English writers of his day, and wrote biographies of Thomas Paine, Thomas Carlyle, and Nathaniel Hawthorne. In the late sixties Walt Whitman entrusted him with a specially amended copy of *Leaves of Grass*, which he brought to William Michael Rossetti who was preparing an English edition. He assisted Rossetti in some of the work. Whether he was paid by Whitman is not known. In 1875 Mark Twain gave him *Tom Sawyer* to place in England. Chatto and Windus took it, and for the next five years Twain conducted his affairs with the firm through Conway, paying him a small fee. The work for both Twain and Whitman could hardly have occupied more than a small portion of Conway's time, and it was perhaps mostly an act of generosity to two admired writers.

IV   Competitors: Newspaper Agencies
and Societies for Authors

GOVERNOR CAPE. Learning useless? Impossible!—Where are the Oxfords, the
Halifaxes, the great protectors and patrons of the liberal arts?

ROBIN. Patron!—The word has lost its use; a guinea subscription at the
request of a lady whose chambermaid is acquainted with the author, may
be now and then picked up——Protectors!—Why I dare believe there's
more money laid out upon Islington Turnpike in a month, than upon all
the learned men in Great Britain in seven years.

GOVERNOR CAPE. And yet the press groans with their productions. How do
they all exist?

ROBIN. In garrets, Sir; as, if you will step to your son's apartment in the next
street, you will see.

—Samuel Foote, *The Author*, 1757

The assorted precursors and prototypes of the true agent suggest
that he was an inevitable phenomenon. In a broad sense this was so.
At the same time, part of the service that he performed might have
been answered by other means. Coming into being in the same years
were the newspaper agencies and the Society of Authors, both of
which served as middlemen between authors and publishers and
competed with the true agents. The newspaper agents originated and
flourished slightly earlier than the true agents; and in the form they
took, they seem more to have assisted than hindered the latter. They
served only part of the publishing world, and they served editors and
publishers instead of authors. They offered an example to follow and
left a gap to fill. They themselves were a consequence of the multi-
plication of newspapers during the century. The *Newspaper Press
Directory* of 1861 reported a total of 1,102 newspapers in the United
Kingdom that year, a rise from 267 in 1821, 295 in 1831, 472 in 1841,
and 563 in 1851. One of the great spurs to newspaper publication
came in 1861 itself with the repeal of the paper tax (following the
repeal of the newspaper and advertisement taxes some years earlier).
The Times immediately reduced its price from $4d$. to $3d$. and its
circulation rose by almost 30 per cent. Many $\frac{1}{2}d$. papers began to be
printed. And by the late sixties the provincial press—which provided
the chief activity for the newspaper agencies—began to give a
prominent role to original fiction. In subsequent years a provincial

weekly might run two or three original serial novels and as many short stories in a single issue. Both newspaper agencies and literary agents began to supply this market.[1]

The first newspaper agencies apparently sprang from the newspaper advertising agencies that came into being early in the century. The firm of Samuel Deacon (in the 1880s publishers of *Deacon's Newspaper Hand Book*) claimed precedence in the advertising field, their records going back to 1822, with the firm in existence some time before that date. An Irishman by the name of Alexander Johnston put in a counterclaim for his father, who started business in 1819. A few years later came Charles Mitchell, who used his connections as an advertising agent to supply literary material to newspapers. He may even have been the first true literary agent. He was born in Norwich in 1807, and as a young man became an advertisement agent for town and country newspapers. His stepgrandson, Edgar Wellsman, describes him as a man about town, a friend particularly of writers and artists, and an amateur actor. From 1836 onwards he was a publisher in Red Lion Court, Fleet Street, from which address he issued books for women, guides to employment in London, and other obscure literature. In 1846 he began publishing his *Newspaper Press Directory*, which in its successive editions has held a pre-eminent place among such directories ever since. He seems to have produced the first edition single-handedly, and it shows him to be a man of some learning and considerable diligence. It was the first such directory of any consequence, and preceded *Willing's Press Guide* (late *May's*) by more than twenty-five years. In an advertisement for it, he said that it was the fruit of almost twenty years of experience with the London and provincial press, and he offered it to publishers, public companies, solicitors, and advertisers 'for the judicious distribution of their announcements'.

1 Original serial fiction had a brief life behind it. Until 1819, when monthly and quarterly magazines were completely exempted from the newspaper tax, very little such fiction had been published, since it rendered magazines liable to taxation. By the 1830s serial fiction was becoming a regular feature of several magazines, and by the 1840s it was often the most important feature. The rise of the part-issue novel followed, and also the introduction of shilling magazines, which began to have circulations in the hundred thousands. (Graham Pollard, 'Serial Fiction', in *New Paths in Book Collecting*, London, 1934.)

Two other advertisements in the first edition are of special interest. One is for a *Guide for the Writing Desk; or, Young Author's and Secretary's Friend.* The *Guide* was published by Mitchell himself, and the compiler is identified as 'T. A.', who wrote it at Mitchell's suggestion. It is largely a discourse on style—perspicuity, purity, propriety, and grammatical nicety—and includes some advice on punctuation, forms of address in letters, and three pages on manuscript correction symbols. It has no odour of vanity publication about it, and indicates a perfectly serious concern for the aspiring writer. The other advertisement is a companion-piece:

> Literary assistance.—A gentleman who has been for some years connected with the London and provincial press, offers his services to revise MSS. and prepare them for the press . . . ; his services would be of advantage to authors, who are not, from experience, *au fait* in the minutiae and details of the publishing department.
>   Address, Alpha, care of Mr. Mitchell. . . .

This experienced gentleman may not have been Mitchell either; but the fact that the advertisement is the only one of its sort suggests that Mitchell may again have been the guiding spirit.

In the next few years, subsequent editions of the *Directory* show Mitchell developing very clearly in the direction of the newspaper agent, less clearly in that of the true literary agent. The literary assistance advertisement disappears from the second edition (1847) and reappears in the third (1851) over the anonym 'Exhibition'. The advertisement for the *Guide* remains. In the 1851 edition there appears an advertisement on the first page that marks the first known use of the term 'literary agency' in such a context.

Literary and Advertising Agency

> To authors, publishers, secretaries of public companies, etc., C. Mitchell . . . begs . . . to call . . . particular attention to that system of *Literary Agency* which he devised so many years since, and has carried out to the satisfaction and advantage of all parties.

The advertisement goes on to mention that he is not only an advertising agent but also a forwarding agent for books, prints, and music for review; and he 'begs to add that he will at all times be happy to give his personal advice to publishers, authors, secretaries .

of public companies, and other advertisers'. This edition also has an article on 'The Advertising Agent', presumably written by Mitchell himself. It describes the advertising agent as a seemingly anomalous middleman but one who serves an invaluable purpose. Imagine how clumsy it would be for a London advertiser to undertake separate negotiations with dozens of provincial papers. Imagine the absurdity of each provincial paper employing an agent to search out advertisers. The independent advertising agent is the answer, the knowledgeable man to whom the advertiser can entrust a sum to spend, the reliable man to whom the newspaper can send the bill. Years later the literary agent would be defended in similar terms.

It is in this third edition too that Mitchell (or his follower) advertises for the first time as a newspaper agent supplying literary material. In the literary assistance advertisement (again the only advertisement of its sort), 'Exhibition' repeats almost verbatim the invitation of 'Alpha', and then adds: 'The advertiser is also prepared to enter into arrangements with the proprietors of country newspapers for the transmission of a weekly letter, containing the latest political, fashionable, musical, literary, and theatrical intelligence of the metropolis.' Such letters had a long history, going back to the origin of newspapers; but if, as seems possible, 'Exhibition' saw his role more as a transmitter of news prepared by others than as a writer of news, his letter would anticipate the activities of the established newspaper agencies later in the century. According to Edgar Wellsman, the proposed letter is of the same description as a 'London Letter' that Mitchell himself supplied perhaps as early as 1845. Nothing more is known of the letter, and little more about Mitchell. The *Morning Post* of 24 March 1851 reported that on his birthday he was given a testimonial dinner by 'upwards of two hundred authors, proprietors, and editors of the provincial press . . . who felt deeply sensible of the services which Mr. Mitchell had rendered their order . . . , establishing a "Literary Agency", by means of which a regular intercommunication between London authors and publishers and the proprietors and editors of the provincial journals is kept up'. He died in 1859. In the following year there appeared in the *Athenaeum* an advertisement from 'A. B. Y.', care of C. Mitchell & Co.', asking for stories for a 'publishing firm of standing' and assuring that 'authorship will be held in confidence if desired'. The assurance of anonymity suggests that provincial newspaper publication may have been intended. If so, newspaper agency was well on its way.

In 1863 the oldest formally established newspaper agency was founded, the Central Press. Beginning in that year, the Press issued a 'newspaper for newspaper proprietors', which consisted of items extracted from *The Times*, the *Illustrated London News*, *Punch*, and other papers in England and abroad. Whether the Press supplied anything else is unknown, and at least until 1879 there was no fiction included in the newspaper. Several other agencies were founded in the seventies and eighties. The one about which most is known was the Tillotson Syndicate, which began operating perhaps as early as 1873. An account of the whole Tillotson firm was written by Frank Singleton, present editor of the *Bolton Evening News*. The firm began as a printing establishment in 1827 in Bolton, Lancashire, and in 1867, under William Frederic Tillotson (1844–89), started to publish newspapers, first and most notably the *Bolton Evening News*, and later several weekly newspapers. Stories were introduced into these papers as a means of boosting circulation; and in order to pay for them, Tillotson invited other newspaper proprietors to publish jointly. Presently the firm found itself a general supplier of fiction to newspapers throughout England. In the late eighties it made a formal international connection with the McClure Syndicate in America, which had been founded around 1884 by S. S. McClure (1857–1949). Established writers were evidently at first reluctant to sell to Tillotsons, thinking that publication in a provincial paper was undignified; but they soon came to terms: prices ranging from £10 to £1,000 and more, book rights reserved to the authors themselves, and incidental advertising of their other wares. In the early nineties Sir Arthur Conan Doyle was getting £5 per thousand words from Tillotsons, and in 1896 he was asking for slightly more than £40 per thousand (£2,500 for a 60,000-word book). He was their highest paid author at the time. They dealt with many authors directly in their early years, and whether they regarded literary agents as an intrusion or a convenience is unknown. Very likely it was the latter—though Sir Philip Gibbs, who worked for Tillotsons for a time, used to speak with pleasure of the 'paltry price' that he himself arranged with Arnold Bennett for *The Grand Babylon Hotel*, which Gibbs foresaw would be the huge success that it was. But Bennett had only a modest reputation at the time, and it is clear from his dealings with the firm shortly thereafter, when he was a client of J. B. Pinker, that neither he nor an agent on his behalf could have obtained a price much beyond the £75 that Tillotsons had paid him little more than a year earlier for his first serial, *Love and Life*. Their initial offer on that book had been £60. Interestingly enough, the Tillotson firm was commonly referred to as a literary agency until at least the turn of the century.

Unlike the newspaper syndicates, the modern Society of Authors was consciously a competitor of the literary agent. The comparable society in France, the *Société des Gens de Lettres*, founded in 1837, did in fact dominate in the role of literary agent for several decades; but the Society of Authors came into being when the agents already had a foothold in England, and even in its heyday the Society did not threaten the agents in a serious way. The Society was the cul-mination of at least a century and a half of organizational efforts to protect authors. One early organization was the Society for the Encouragement of Learning, founded in 1735 for the purpose of sec-uring for authors a rightful share in the profits of their books. The membership seems to have consisted of high-minded gentlemen who solved the problem by becoming publishers themselves and giving their authors all the rewards. Among other works they published an edition of Newton's *Quadrature of Curves*, printed by James Bettenham and sold by John Nourse of Temple Bar and John Whiston of Fleet Street, booksellers to the Society. Since Newton had been dead for eighteen years when the book was published, in 1845, the Society was presumably encouraging learning more than it was encouraging authors. All the same, the Society ruffled the nerves of the commercial bookseller-publishers, and in 1738 there appeared a tract in their defence, *A Letter to the Society of Book-sellers*. The anonymous author remarks upon the 'great complaints . . . made daily against you', notably that you pocket all or most of the profits on a book; but the author thinks that there is nothing in the charge or at least that there is no reason why a writer should not be able to bargain well. He does acknowledge that publishers' customary means of choosing books—obtaining the opinion of a respected person—is inadequate, and he laments that as a writer himself he has never been able to find a friend willing or able to give disinterested advice. He does not think the Society for the Encouragement of Learning is the answer. The Society itself lasted some eleven years, the ideals of the members apparently having been better than their business sense.

In 1825 a similar organization had a brief life, the Society for the Encouragement of Literature. The Society viewed with pleasure the immense profit to be made from books, and thought that by operating on a strictly cash basis they could provide pensions for their authors and greater immediate rewards all round, for themselves as well. They expected to do the purchasing of copyrights and then print and publish through ordinary channels. This venture seems likewise to have foundered within a few years. In 1838 a National Association for the Encouragement and Protection of Authors, and Men of Talent and Genius issued a prospectus of a publishing society that aimed to avoid quarrelling with the booksellers. The prime mover of the Association, William Jerdan, examined the records of the Society for the Encouragement of Learning in the British Museum, and he reported that it was the booksellers who had destroyed that Society a century earlier—indeed the very booksellers who served the Society, for they charged exorbitant commissions for their services. He thought that in these latter days, when such wickedness could more readily be held up to the public light, there would be less trouble of this sort. And there may have been. But whether the Association ever got beyond its prospectus is unknown. In 1843 one more scheme of the same sort was elaborated by John Petheram, writer and second-hand bookdealer (to whom the young John Camden Hotten, founder of Chatto and Windus, was later apprenticed), in his *Reasons for Establishing an Author's Publication Society*. All well-known authors of both sexes would belong, and anyone else who wanted to. The Society would operate in the manner of the recently formed Camden Society, issuing books to members at less than half the ordinary price. It would especially benefit young authors by giving them a sympathetic publisher and audience. Petheram calculated that under conventional publishing methods—with trade discounts and remaindering—retail prices were as much as three times the real price; and in consequence both authors and public were badly served. Two years earlier, Petheram reported, he had taken his proposal to an eminent author, who was uninterested in it, and he now offered it to the world. The world seems to have been equally uninterested.

An enterprise of another sort was the Royal Literary Fund, founded in 1790, whose service was not primarily to find or be a generous publisher but to salve the wounds of the author in his long quarrel. The founder, David Williams, was so 'affected by the calamitous fortunes of authors, which were daily recurring to his observations' that as early as 1773 he proposed his ideas to a literary society of which he was a member. But his friends apparently showed no concern until the late eighties, when the scholar and translator Floyer Sydenham was arrested for a small debt to his victualler, and died in prison as a consequence. The constitution of the Fund was published in 1790, and argued as perhaps the most important reason for aiding authors in distress that to do so would prevent them from turning satirical and calumniating princes. Whether in consequence or not, the Fund presently came under royal favour, and in 1818 received its Royal Charter of Incorporation. In an account of the Fund a few years later, some notice was taken of the bookseller-publisher as the author's agent:

> . . . it has been asserted that our proceedings are unnecessary—that the reward of an author is immediately connected with his merit; and that the bookseller as the agent between him and the public supersedes the expediency of our own interference on his behalf. Would to Heaven that this assertion were as true as it is specious.

The course of the Fund in the nineteenth century was not altogether successful, and its policies were the subject of occasional attack, how well justified is unclear. In 1833 Richard Henry Horne, novelist, essayist, and editor, published his *Exposition of the False Medium and Barriers Excluding Men of Genius from the Public*. He recommended in it the forming of a society to encourage literature, and in doing so he attacked the record of the Royal Literary Fund.

Part of his comment summarized the case of Robert Heron, which Isaac D'Israeli had described in *Calamities of Authors*. On 2 February 1807 Heron addressed a letter to the Fund from a lock-up house in Chancery Lane, where he was in confinement for debt. The letter recounts a literary career that began in Edinburgh when Heron was eleven years old (in 1775) and 'mingled with my studies the labour of teaching or of writing, to support and educate myself'. During the next twenty years he did a great deal of translating and published accounts of the history and topography of Scotland and of the life of Burns. In 1799 he came to London, where he wrote and published voluminously. 'I can prove', he said, 'that I have, for many years, read and written, one day with another, from twelve to sixteen hours a day. As a human being, I have not been free from follies and errors, but the tenor of my life has been temperate, laborious, humble, quiet, and, to the utmost of my power, beneficent.' And the consequence of this virtue: 'For these last ten months I have been brought to the very extremity of bodily and pecuniary distress. I shudder at the thought of perishing in a gaol.' D'Israeli reported that an investigating physician found Heron's health so deteriorated from the 'indiscreet exertion of his mind, in protracted and incessant literary labours' that there was no possibility of his paying his debts. Three months later Heron died in Newgate. D'Israeli used the case merely to dilate upon the condition of authorship:

O ye populace of scribblers! before ye are driven to a garret, and your eyes are filled with constant tears, pause—recollect that not one of you possesses the learning or the abilities of Heron; shudder at all this secret agony and silent perdition!

Horne, in contrast, belaboured the Literary Fund for failing to respond to Heron's plea, and he instanced other authors who might have been helped but were not. His book prompted an extended review-article in the pages of the *Literary Gazette*, much of which was devoted to a defence of the Fund. The reviewer was possibly William Jerdan, who ran the *Gazette*. As a contributor to the Fund, the reviewer saw fit to look at the records, and he found that three days after Heron had written his letter, the founder of the Fund, David Williams himself, had carried £20 to Heron. It was true, said the reviewer, that Heron died later that year, true also that more money might have been provided; but the Fund had little money at the time, Heron was not the most distinguished and deserving of literary figures, and the rules of the Fund usually required the author to present himself at the offices of the Fund to receive his money.

Later in the century Charles Dickens attacked the administrators of the Fund, charging that rather a large proportion of the income of the Fund went for annual dinners in honour of literature. In 1858 the income was £1,225 and the expenses of management were above £500, roughly 40 per cent. He also reported that widows of prosperous members sometimes received grants of £100 while other applicants were turned down or offered £5. One of the administrators a few years later was Anthony Trollope, who was apparently satisfied with the conduct of affairs if not with the adequacy of help. He remarks in his *Autobiography* that as an administrator 'I heard and saw much of the sufferings of authors', and he later says that 'the experience I have acquired . . . forbids me to advise any young man or woman to enter boldly on a literary career in search of bread. I know how utterly I should have failed myself had my bread not been earned elsewhere while I was making my efforts.' Forty years later Arnold Bennett attacked the Fund on grounds similar to Dickens's.

An indirect benefit of the Fund when it first attracted royal attention may have been the founding of the Royal Society of Literature in 1820–1 under the auspices of George IV. The Society declined with the King's death in 1830, King William IV indicating that he was too poor to support it; but in its few years the Society provided annual grants of one hundred guineas to each of ten Royal Associates, and by this means helped to relieve the burden of Coleridge's last years. There were also two medals awarded annually, and in the fourth year Sir Walter Scott and Robert Southey won them.

The latter part of the nineteenth century saw considerable efforts by authors to organize themselves. In 1851 the Guild of Literature and Art was founded to 'sustain from despair the youth of a future Chatterton' and to support the old age of others. 'The day . . . has come', said the Guild, 'when civilization should no longer forget the civilizers.' Sir Edward Bulwer Lytton was prime mover and President of the Guild, and Dickens was Vice-President. Both these men had been involved, along with Carlyle, Thackeray, and others, in an abortive attempt to found a similar society in 1843; and Dickens had eventually to write the epitaph of the new organization in his dedication of *Bleak House* 'as a remembrance of our friendly union to my companions in the Guild'. The Guild operated as an insurance and provident society, using the services of the National Provident Institution. Its significant aim was to provide 'salaries' and housing for needy and deserving members. The salaries ranged from £100 to £200 a year, and the houses were on land at Stevenage, Hertfordshire, given by Bulwer Lytton. The persons aided were expected in return to give one or more public lectures a year—by proxy if need be. The Guild began auspiciously, raising over £3,000 in benefit performances of plays written for the occasion by Bulwer Lytton and Dickens, and acted in by Dickens, Wilkie Collins, John Forster, John Tenniel, and others. Sir Edwin Landseer designed scenery. But the Guild languished. The cottages were not ready until 1865. Eight years later the *Publishers' Circular* gleefully reported that no one had yet been found willing to live in them.

Two years later, some of the same people were involved in the formation of the Association to Protect the Rights of Authors, whose interest seems mainly to have been to improve copyright laws. A group of members discussed the matter with the Prime Minister, Disraeli. Apparently little more was done. Then eight years later came the Society of Authors. The Society began with three announced aims: (1) the maintenance, definition, and defence of literary property, (2) the consolidation and amendment of the laws of domestic copyright, and (3) the promotion of international copyright. With the experience of others as a warning, they decided to begin from a position of power, and persuaded Tennyson to be President and Matthew Arnold, Thomas Henry Huxley, Charles Reade, and Wilkie Collins to be Vice-Presidents. In 1884 the Society had sixty-eight members. Eight years later they had more than 900; and by 1914 they had 2,500. In 1889 the Society sponsored the Authors' Syndicate, a non-profit literary agency. Some account of the Syndicate is given on pages 55–6. The following year the

Society began publishing the *Author*, a monthly, which for many years thereafter was a militant voice in behalf of authors' rights. Its editor was Sir Walter Besant, who was the mainstay of the Society itself and who thoroughly enjoyed the battle with the publishers. The pages of the *Author* were inadequate for him, and he carried the attack into the *Athenaeum*, the *Illustrated London News*, and other journals.

Curiously enough, the *Author* was almost as hostile to literary agents as it was to publishers. A. P. Watt printed the journal for the Society, advertised in it, was a prominent figure at annual banquets of the Society, and served as Besant's own agent from 1884 onwards, receiving an expression of deep gratitude in Besant's *Autobiography*. No matter. The hostility survived Besant, and continued until the late 1930s. In the first years of the journal, every issue reported a story of a hapless author being victimized by a publisher or an agent. The *Author* held up to an unkind light such firms as the Authors' Advice Bureau and the Authors' Publishing Association, wanting to know the literary qualifications and publishing experience of the people who ran them. It reported on a London Literary Society which guaranteed to find a publisher for certain authors and fulfilled the guarantee by using its fees to print a magazine full of the authors' stories. (Here was the literary agent as vanity publisher.) Besant himself took note of an advertisement in the *Daily News* in which an already published writer offered a 25 per cent commission to someone who could place two manuscripts. The advertiser was misguided, said Besant, and ought to save himself money by getting advice through the Society of Authors. An article on literary agents in 1892 argued that it was absurd to imagine that an agent could sell what the writer himself could not. Occasionally the *Author* admitted that there were reliable agents and even recommended that writers find one, but on the next page was the suggestion that the Society could serve them better. So things went for many years. Had the Society come into existence earlier and had its own literary agency been more competent, the role of the independent agent might not have proved so dominant. As it was, most authors seem to have developed a double allegiance: to the Society of Authors as a broad instrument of power and to their individual agents as the efficient instruments of work. And some authors, as a matter of fact, looked with a measure of disdain upon the Society. In 1890 J. M. Barrie examined the contents of the second issue of the *Author* and found that it served literary aspirants rather more than authors; Andrew Lang sniped at the Society throughout the nineties; and a few years later Hume Nisbet wrote a small book attacking the Society, the Authors' Syndicate, the *Author*, and the Authors' Club (founded by Besant) for their smugness, crassness, and incompetence.

V   The First Agents: Paterson, Poles, Burghes, Watt, Colles, Pinker, Brown, and Others

> Accursed the man, whom fate ordains, in spite,
> And cruel parents teach, to read and write!
> —Charles Churchill, *The Author*, 1764

By such a variety of precursors was the way prepared for the true literary agent, the man who was ready to earn a living serving the interests of several authors among several publishers. Doubtless many of the precursors came close to being true agents, but lacked the gall to charge their friends a fee or lacked the talent or interest to develop their opportunity in more than a casual or limited way. As a group, the vanity publishers may have come closest. They should have searched more carefully for good authors, and resisted the easy reward of doing the publishing themselves on commission. Doubtless one of the precursors did transform himself into the first true agent, but who he was and what he was are unknown. Very possibly, though, he discovered his vocation by reading the advertisements of vanity publishers and authors' accountants on the front page of the *Athenaeum* in the middle of the century. Here are two such advertisements from the year 1845.

Just published, with 8 engravings, price 1*s.*, *The Author's Hand-Book*; a guide to the art and system of publishing on commission. 'We can recommend this as a good *vade mecum* for ladies and gentlemen intending to publish their own works. It is most elegantly printed and embellished and contains a list of the cost of printing, paper, binding, etc.'—Bell's Messenger.

To authors and publishers: Mr. Joseph Jackson (late of Sambrook Court), arbitrator and accountant, having had many years' experience of agreements and accounts, between authors and publishers, offers his services to adjust disputed and partnership accounts. . . .

In 1850 appeared an advertisement that may have been by a true agent:

To publishers and amateur authors—the author of numerous works, historical and imaginative, is desirous of employment as a reader to a publisher, editor of a periodical, and in preparing manuscripts for the press, in which occupation he has had many years' experience in one of the first publishing houses in London. His assistance would be found of great advantage to noblemen or gentlemen having any work in progress, which he would not only carefully revise, but would negotiate its publication, and correct the proof sheets. Address, prepaid, to A. B., care of Charles Mears, Esq., 9 Westbourne Place, Eaton Square.

Who A. B. and Charles Mears were is unknown, except that Mears (also Meers and Meeres) was at this address for at least fifteen years. The framing of the latter part of the advertisement suggests that the advertiser might have been a disguised agent of a vanity publisher. If so, it shows that the vanity publisher was close enough to being a true agent to think of describing himself as one. Otherwise it implies almost the same thing: that literary agency arose in emulation of vanity publication, the first agent addressing his appeal to a typical customer of the vanity publisher, offering the same easy path to publication, and assuming all the incidental burdens.

In 1855 appeared an advertisement with a narrower range: 'Authors—a publisher of standing wants a good novel. He will pay £100 for the one he selects. . . . Address letters and packets to "Liber", care of Mr. S. Deacon, 154 Leadenhall Street.' Again the situation is unclear. 'Liber' may be a publisher's agent, operating in a more public and indiscriminate way than such agents usually operated. He may be a vanity publisher baiting his hook. He may be an author's agent displaying one of the necessary contacts among publishers that an author's agent needs. Or he may be Samuel Deacon himself, the newspaper advertising agent, looking for something for the provincial press. At least until 1851, when he was at another address, Deacon kept a coffee- and boarding-house as well as his agency, and invited country gentlemen to stay there. In any event, the advertisement again suggests literary agency.

Such advertisements as these increased over the years, and others of an encouraging sort appeared along with them. Newspaper agencies began to advertise for stories, individual magazines did likewise, and numerous literary assistants offered to help literary aspirants to revise their work. In 1859 James Lowe, editor of the

Critic, remarked upon the profusion of people connected with the book trade who were advertising their willingness to consult with young authors. And in June 1870 appeared an advertisement of a firm that identified itself as a true literary agency:

The London Literary Agency, instituted to facilitate intercourse between authors and publishers, and to supply the provincial press with literary and political matter. Manuscripts examined and advised upon; books seen through the press; pamphlets prepared on any subject; translations made; and literary business of every kind promptly and efficiently managed. Prospectus on application. Offices, 23 Tavistock Street, Covent Garden.

Unfortunately the firm and its manager remain unknown, and the little information available hardly supports conjecture on them. From 1866 to February 1870 the *Court Circular*, a weekly journal for fashionable people, was issued from 23 Tavistock Street. Its publisher from 1866 to March 1869 was Alfred Edwin Rawlinson, and then the firm of George Maddick took over. The *Post Office Directory* gives the *Court Circular* at the address, with Rawlinson as publisher, from 1866 through 1870, and after that date it lists a ship and insurance broker. Rawlinson does not seem to have edited any other London periodicals before or after these dates, and nothing else could be discovered about him. He might have been the first nameable agent, but he avoided fame, and the agency seems to have died quickly.

The first nameable agent is in fact hard to identify. For in the seventies, when the phrase 'literary agent' began to come into general currency, some of the persons who called themselves agents were perhaps simply revising manuscripts or ghost-writing. This may be the case with the two agents who appear in the first listing of *Agents—literary* in the *Post Office Directory* of 1874. They are Paterson and Vary, 2 King's Road, and Stefan Poles, 20 Great Marlborough Street. Paterson and Vary were in the *Directory* for a single year, and their first names remain undiscovered; but it would seem that they were one man named Thomas Vary Paterson (1811–80). He was a writer and journalist, and worked for a while in America, where he apparently gained some reputation. He was the author of booklets called *The Art of Living; or, Good Advice for the Old and Young* (1875) and *How to Get Money Quickly; or, Thirty Ways of Making a Fortune* (1868). Inside the cover of the latter booklet he advertises a 'London Literary Bureau and Agency', which proposes thirty ways by which he himself can make a fortune. He will write or revise bills, pamphlets, lectures, debates, sermons, tracts, biographies, essays, and tales, on poetry, sculpture, travel, adventure, science, agriculture, horticulture, physiology, education, and any other topic of interest. The booklet itself, surprisingly enough, is a patchwork of sardonic paragraphs on human greed. Paterson suggests that one way for a man to make a fortune is to go out to Australia and send back stories about digging up forty-pound gold nuggets. The newspapers will play up the stories to help circulation, and there will be a flood of emigration. The man will buy and sell land wisely, and will eventually 'return to England . . . in possession of that which gives a man *worth and honour* when living, and a Christian obituary after he is dead'. The advertised agency may well be part of the satire. Seven years later Paterson perhaps fell upon hard times. His *Art of Living* consists of bits and pieces offered straightforwardly, and the brief death notice of him in *The Times* in 1880 speaks of a lingering illness. What sort of agency he was prepared to conduct in 1874 is anyone's guess.

The same must be said of Stefan Poles (also Stefen Polhès; 1847?–75), who appeared in the *Directory* for 1876 as well as for 1874 and 1875. In his own time he was a mysterious figure. According to one account he was born in Poland, educated in Bavaria, and as a young man participated in revolutionary activity against Russia; he was condemned to death and fled Poland in 1864. Another account implies that his real name was Tugenhold and that he was a Polish traitor, serving as a Russian spy. In the middle sixties he published three books on Poland, two of them issued in Sweden and the other in Germany. Later he seems to have gone to America as a newspaperman. In 1870 he was in France, reportedly to raise a regiment of Poles to fight the Prussians; he was intimate with the Communists in 1871, imprisoned at Versailles for several months, and at the end of the year escaped to England. Of his years in England little is known except that for a time he was a photographer's assistant and later he was involved in legal wrangles. Early in 1874 he won a suit against *The Times*, which had accused him of trying to extort money from Louis Adolphe Thiers and of misrepresenting himself as a *Times* correspondent. Later that year he successfully sued the printer and publisher of a pamphlet in which he was libelled by 'supposed Polish patriots' (in his own phrase). A copy of the pamphlet was brought illegally into the British Museum, and Poles wrote threatening letters to the Chief Librarian, Winter Jones, in an effort to have it removed. Jones was unresponsive, and Poles then wrote a pamphlet, *The Actual Condition of the British Museum*, published in February or March 1875, which included his exchanges with Jones and among other things compared the underground working rooms of the Museum to his prison cell at Versailles—and with some good evidence. He died about 22 November. The only known obituary notice, in the *World*, may have been inspired by his enemies:

A waif.—The flame of a strong, wayward, mysterious life has been snuffed out. Stefan Poles . . . has died miserably in Middlesex Hospital, friendless and raving in an unknown tongue, and been buried by charity. A photograph of the ghastly unshaven face, with the glazed left eye still open, was taken after death. It bore a strange resemblance to one Tugenhold, a 'converted' Jew and Russian spy, son to the Chief Rabbi of Warsaw, who was censor of the press there previous to the last uprising.

The other literary agents listed in the *Post Office Directory* in the six years following the first appearance of Paterson and Poles are equally unsubstantial as agents. From 1874 to 1894 the Directory listed a total of nineteen agents in London. In all these years no more than six agents were listed at one time, and as late as 1891 only two appeared. Except for three men, none of them survived more than four years; and one of those three, Henry Stevens of Vermont, never seems to have been a literary agent in the conventional sense of the word. The other two were A. M. Burghes and A. P. Watt, who are the first nameable agents known to be true agents. They also happen to be the first discovered true agents who advertised publicly. On 18 March 1882 and on subsequent dates in the *Athenaeum*, Burghes advertised as an 'authors' agent and accountant. Advice given as to the best mode of publishing. Publishers' accounts and estimates examined on behalf of authors. Transfer of literary property carefully conducted.' And on 2 December 1882 and sub-sequent dates, Watt begged to announce 'to authors and publishers that he had been appointed by Herr Karl Graedener, of Hamburg, his literary agent in England with full powers to negotiate the pur-chase of English works suitable for Asher's Collection of English Authors'. Both advertisements indicate that the true agent was pre-pared to be other things as well.

Little is known of Alexander Macleod Burghes. He exemplifies the shadowy, shady side of literary agency in its earliest days—a side as important as the respectable side in the origins of agency, and equally so in the argument over agency in later years. He first appeared in the *Post Office Directory* in 1881 as an accountant, with offices at 12 and 14 Catherine Street, the address also of Edward Curtice, a wholesale news dealer, who in the mid-eighties became a literary agent briefly. The following year he moved to 1A Paternoster Row. In another advertisement in the *Athenaeum*, two months be-fore he offered his services as an author's agent, he described himself as a publisher's manager who could accept a few more manuscripts for the spring season. Perhaps he was in part a front for vanity publishers. Other advertisements during 1882 said that he had twenty-five years of experience, or sometimes twenty years. An advertisement a few years later mentioned that he had been chief clerk to the publishing house of Rivington for ten years. His first listing as a literary agent in the *Post Office Directory* was in 1884. After the turn of the century he moved to 34 Paternoster Row, where Watt had been in 1882. Among his clients listed in the *Literary Year-Book* in 1911 were Ouida, W. Robertson Nicoll, Moberly Bell (editor of *The Times*), and a host of unknown writers. Perhaps Ouida learned her dislike of agents from him; and Nicoll, who was a friend of A. P. Watt, could hardly have been a client for long. He was reported in 1911 to have founded his agency in 1879. In 1912, when he was seventy, he was prosecuted for the fraudulent conversion of £50. A woman gave him the sum to pay to the publisher John Ouseley as a subsidy for her book. He did not for-ward the money, and later told her that the book was being held over till the next season. In court he admitted the charge, and traced the theft to a broken ankle he had suffered two years before. The ankle had caused him to leave the agency in the hands of his son for a time, and when he eventually returned to work he found himself in financial difficulties. The court accepted his plea of guilty. In the very same month his son was prosecuted on other charges. An author who submitted a manuscript to the firm in 1905 and paid a five-guinea fee for services was later told that the manuscript was lost and given a refund of two guineas. In 1912 the author saw his book being advertised by Ouseley, and thereupon went to law. The younger Burghes maintained in court that the publishing house of David Nutt had sent him the manuscript early in 1912 saying that the elder Burghes had submitted it some time before, and that his father had then told him that the manuscript had been purchased outright from the author. Under such circumstances the younger Burghes felt free to offer the manuscript to Ouseley. The court found the younger Burghes guilty too. The agency of father and son seems to have collapsed therewith.

Of A. P. Watt more is known, partly through Nicoll. He was born in Glasgow in 1834, and grew up in Edinburgh. He was self-educated, and apparently made his living for a time as a bookseller in Edinburgh. He was, says Nicoll, addicted to books. He married the sister of the publisher Alexander Strahan, and later joined Strahan in London as his assistant. Strahan himself was about three years older than Watt, and by the time he was thirty was a well-known publisher (unconnected with the famous eighteenth-century house of the same name). He founded *Good Words* in 1860, *Argosy* in 1865, the *Contemporary Review* in 1866, and some other journals, chiefly of a religious sort. In 1863 *Good Words* had a circulation of 100,000; and the *Contemporary Review*, first under the editorship of Dean Alford and then of J. T. Knowles, attained a European reputation. Strahan's chief author for many years was George MacDonald, best remembered today for *At the Back of the North Wind*. He also published Tennyson for a time, paying him a pre-arranged sum of £4,000 or more a year. At the beginning of his success, in 1862, he moved his office from Edinburgh to London, and presumably Watt joined the firm after that date. Both men lived in Blackheath, and Watt came to know Tennyson, MacDonald, Norman Macleod, and many other literary and religious figures who wrote for Strahan.

Watt developed a friendship with MacDonald that was, says Nicoll, 'one of the warmest and tenderest I have ever known'.

Watt served as Strahan's secretary, reader of manuscripts, and head of advertising. Eventually, in 1876, he was taken into partnership. By this time, though, the firm was in financial difficulties—to some extent because of Strahan's generosity to his authors—and either the partnership was little more than nominal or Watt abandoned the post almost as soon as he took it. As early as 1870 Strahan had mortgaged the copyrights to the *Contemporary Review* and other journals to secure a loan. Seven years later J. T. Knowles seceded from the *Contemporary Review* to edit the new *Nineteenth Century*, which was controlled by the same people who held Strahan's mortgages and who apparently intended to strangle the *Contemporary Review*. Strahan went to court against the mortgage holders who were refusing to surrender the mortgages upon payment prior to the due date. He won his case, but the *Contemporary Review* presently passed into the hands of a limited company. Strahan's firm rapidly declined. Watt's first recourse when the firm ran into trouble was to become an advertising agent, in which business, according to Nicoll, he had considerable success and little pleasure. He then became a literary agent. The date that he became a literary agent is uncertain and the evidence is contradictory, partly because he must have acted occasionally and informally before he committed himself fully. His firm today gives the date as 1875, and says that he is known to have acted earlier. George MacDonald, who was by all accounts Watt's first client, wrote in 1892 that more than ten years had passed since Watt became his agent. Watt himself in an interview with 'F. W.' (possibly the publisher F. V. White) in the *Bookman* in 1892 put the date at 1878:

When I started to sell copyrights some fourteen years ago, the literary agent was an unknown factor in the world of letters. My friend, Dr. George MacDonald, asked me to sell his stories, which I did—and I think I may say with much success. Dr. MacDonald found that my acting in his behalf in this way relieved him of an immense deal of trouble and worry, and he then, and has ever since, placed the management of his literary affairs entirely under my care. At the time I was doing this for him it occurred to me that other authors might be glad to be relieved of what Mr. Besant has called 'the intolerable trouble of haggling and bargaining', and one author recommending my services to another—for I never advertise, you know—I gradually came to occupy the position I now hold.

Watt's recollection of the date would accord with his having become Strahan's partner in 1876 and then having abandoned the firm to become an advertising agent. However, one of the biographies of Wilkie Collins, who presumably became a client after MacDonald, seems to imply that Collins was consulting Watt as early as 1875. Without doubt Collins was with Watt by 1879. The situation is further complicated by the fact that until 1886 Watt and Strahan were both at 34 Paternoster Row, where Strahan had been since 1876. Watt first appeared in the trades directory of the *Post Office Directory* as an advertising agent in 1880, and the street directory continued to list him solely as an advertising agent until at least 1890. He first appeared in the trades directory as a literary agent in 1881, three years before Burghes.

Whatever the date was that Watt first acted as a literary agent, he gradually established himself with many of the famous writers of the day, and the testimonial letters that they wrote to him are indeed a remarkable tribute, indicating not only that he became the friend of several writers, tripled their incomes, and saved them worry, but fundamentally that he answered a great need. As one writer put it in a letter to the firm some years after his death: had Watt begun his agency years earlier, Isaac D'Israeli would never have been able to write about the calamities of authors. Of course there must have been sour notes—notes that never got written, such as one from Henry James, who tried Watt and found him wanting. And not every reader of the book of testimonial letters was impressed, even when he was an author instead of a publisher. Watt sent Joseph Conrad a copy shortly after the turn of the century, as an invitation to become a client. Conrad wrote to J. B. Pinker that the book put him in mind of the credentials of his Malayan laundrywoman. There is, too, the fact that the first edition of the book followed hard upon the interview in 1892 in which Watt disdained advertising. Watt began soliciting the letters as early as 1883, and presumably used them informally until 1893, when he printed what seems to be the first edition.

Despite apparently rapid success, Watt's path was not altogether easy. He had in the first place to invent his fee. According to the firm today, he began by charging a lawyer's fee for letter-writing, telegraphic expenses, and the like; but he found that his clients did not always pay him, and he decided to obtain payment before the author did. He did eventually adopt a flat fee of 10 per cent of royalties, a figure common among advertisers and one that he himself must have used. The royalty was paid by the publisher through him, and the author received payment minus 10 per cent. The figure remains to this day the basic fee of literary agents in England and America. A more difficult problem was the approach to the publisher. The fact that Strahan was a leading publisher in the sixties gave Watt an entrée that he would otherwise have been denied, and he himself must have known many publishers personally before he became an agent. Even so, the doors of at least one or two publishers were shut to him, and the reception elsewhere was often grudging. His obvious strategy might have seemed to be to say: Well, if you won't have me, you won't have Rudyard Kipling or William Butler Yeats, whose works are handled by me. Such a threat probably played the most important role in bringing the publishers round, so that they eventually regarded the agent as a most agreeable and necessary fellow. But it was a threat best left unspoken by the individual agent, especially in his early years when his empire was small and unstable; and Watt seems to have opened most doors by being capable, hardworking, and diplomatic. Nicoll describes him in these terms, and adds that he was also a very retiring and religious man. Mrs. Belloc Lowndes, who knew him from girlhood onwards, spoke of him as 'a man of outstanding intellectual gifts and integrity'. Some of the publishers, in fact, welcomed him. Andrew Chatto, Sr., was one; F. V. White another. But the pleasant interview in the *Bookman* between Watt and 'F. W.' did not indicate that the battle had been largely won by 1892. The *Bookman* was run by friend Nicoll.

Part of Watt's shrewdness or good fortune was that he acted for publishers as well as for authors. One of his regular activities, at least in his early years, was to sell book rights for a publisher when the publisher could not dispose of them himself. A letter from

Chatto and Windus in 1885 thanked him for arranging serial publication of stories owned by them. His main activities consisted in placing works of authors, executing contracts, collecting royalties, and valuing literary property. By the nineties or earlier he was arranging sales to many American magazines. Nicoll says that he was acquainted with the periodicals of the whole British Empire, had an uncanny instinct for what was good and what would sell, and during most of his career read every manuscript that came into his growing office. In the early nineties he asserted that his interest was as much the unknown author as the known one, though the emphasis seems gradually to have shifted to the latter. One of his peripheral activities was as a publisher. In addition to printing the *Author* for the Society of Authors, he published books on language, the Bible, and Palestine, along with a translation of Rabelais. In the first issue of the *Author*, in 1890, he advertised as a publisher. There were no other advertisements in that radical magazine except by Chatto and Windus, Whitaker's, Elkin Mathews, and George Bell.

For twenty-five years Watt quite thoroughly dominated the profession of literary agency. He was not the first agent, as has been long supposed, but he was the first person with any sort of public reputation to undertake such work systematically, and for a good many years he was apparently the only one. From the seventies until the late eighties he stood alone in contrast to the anonymous or shadowy figures such as Burghes. And from the late eighties until 1896, when J. B. Pinker opened his office, he had only one or two well-known competitors. Literary agency would have flourished and attained respectability without him, but he was in fact the first person under whom it did flourish and attain respectability. When the great rush of agency activity came in the nineties, his example made the way comparatively easy for the men thirty years his junior. When he died in 1914, most publishers wrote letters of condolence to the family.

Among the few agents in England who attained any prominence before 1900, William Morris Colles was the best known after Watt. He was born in 1855, took his degree at Cambridge in 1877, was admitted to the Bar in 1880, and around 1883 was on the staff of the *Standard*. He began his Authors' Syndicate in 1889 (or possibly

1890) and at the same time joined the Council of the Society of Authors. His office was at 4 Portugal Street, along with that of the Society, with whom his firm was initially associated. He also served as legal counsel to the Society. At one time or another he acted for Thomas Hardy and George Meredith, both of whom were Presidents of the Society. The early advertisements of the firm indicate that the management was voluntary and unpaid, and that the Syndicate's services were available only to members of the Society of Authors. The situation seems to have changed a few years later. Colles is described in Frederic Whyte's book on William Heinemann as 'a big, burly, bearded lawyer, with a wheezy infectious laugh—a sort of well-spoken, decent-minded, entirely reputable, nineteenth-century Falstaff'. He was less impressive as an agent, and it may have been because of his incompetence that the Society of Authors failed to establish itself as a literary agency on at least equal terms with the private agencies. He had difficulties with all the writers whose dealings with him are known in any detail—Arnold Bennett, Eden Phillpotts, Murray Gilchrist, and Somerset Maugham. Bennett recorded in his journal a favourable reaction to Colles when the two men met in May 1898 to arrange for Bennett to become a client, but their correspondence over the next four years contains complaints by Bennett and apologies by Colles over the way Bennett's manuscripts are being handled. Bennett too often found himself advising Colles of the proper markets and prices for things. The relationship ended acrimoniously in 1902, some months after Bennett had arranged for J. B. Pinker to handle his work. Letters of the next few years between Bennett and Phillpotts remark with some amusement upon Colles's troubles with his clients. In later years Colles's position declined. He died in 1926.

Another early agent was J. Eveleigh Nash, born in 1873. He came to London in 1892, travelled for Messrs. Warne for several years, and became an agent in 1898, with offices in Norfolk Street and then Arundel Street, the homes also of the Watt and Pinker firms for many years. He acted for about fifteen writers, including Morley Roberts, but abandoned the profession in two years to become an adviser to Constable. Later he was a publisher, perhaps best known for *Nash's Magazine*. In his Memoirs, *I Liked the Life I Lived*, Nash recalls A. P. Watt telling him that George Smith of Smith, Elder said, 'Mr Watt, I believe you can tell a book by the smell of it'; and Nash adds, 'I think Mr. Smith was right'.

The most important English agent after Watt was James Brand Pinker. He was perhaps the most impressive of all the early agents, and a collection of letters testifying to his astuteness, generosity, and energy exists in the correspondence of Henry James, Joseph Conrad, Arnold Bennett, Stephen Crane, Ford Madox Ford, and other writers. (This is to say nothing of some disgruntlement by James Joyce and a characterization of him by D. H. Lawrence as a 'little parvenu snob of a procureur of books'.) Frank Swinnerton describes him thus:

He was short, compact, a rosy, round-faced clean-shaven grey-haired sphinx with a protrusive under-lip, who drove four-in-hand, spoke distinctly in a hoarse voice that was almost a whisper, shook hands shoulder-high, laughed without moving, knew the monetary secrets of authors and the weaknesses of publishers, terrified some of these last and was refused admittance by others, dominated editors, and of course enjoyed much power. . . . He said candidly to one publisher over a contract made direct with the author: 'But this is swindling!' 'Oh!' protested the publisher, 'that's a very strong word!' Pinker fixed those immovable eyes upon his victim. 'What other do you suggest?' 'Well', said the publisher, 'I admit it was sharp practice.' And so the contract was destroyed.

Pinker was born in 1863, and until he began his agency in January 1896 he was a newspaper and magazine editor, working first on the *Levant Herald* in Constantinople and then as assistant editor on *Black and White* in London and briefly as editor of *Pearson's Magazine*, also in London. He seems to have gained a considerable reputation before he became an agent, for among his first clients were H. G. Wells, Oscar Wilde, and Stephen Crane, and by 1901 he was acting for Henry James, Joseph Conrad, and Arnold Bennett. All the same, though, he seems to have given special attention to unknown writers, and the files of the firm contain vast quantities of correspondence with obscure writers. In doing so, he acted not only in contrast to A. P. Watt but also against the trend of agency work. From early days onwards, Watt's advertisements in literary yearbooks listed fifty famous clients he served or quoted the praise of one or another famous client. Pinker's advertisement read: 'Mr. Pinker has always made a special point of helping young authors in the early stages of their career, when they need most the aid of an adviser with a thorough knowledge of the literary world and the publishing trade.'

Pinker's two great successes were Conrad and Bennett, the one the very example of the hapless, impractical writer, the other a man who himself was an excellent informal agent for George Sturt, Pauline Smith, and other writers. On occasion Conrad saw his situation clearly enough. At the outset of his relationship with Pinker, in 1899, when he was of very questionable commercial worth, he wrote to him: 'My method of writing is so unbusinesslike that I don't think you could have any use for such an unsatisfactory person. I generally sell a work before it is begun, get paid when it is half done and don't do the other half till the spirit moves me. I must add that I have no control whatever over the spirit—neither has the man who paid the money.' Pinker took the letter in his stride. He may also have been aware during the ensuing months that Conrad looked with some condescension upon his literary acumen. Four years later Conrad wrote of Pinker to Edmund Gosse when it was being bruited about that Pinker was treating him shabbily—and Gosse perhaps had some hand in the rumour:

He has stepped gallantly into the breach left open by the collapse of my bank: and not only gallantly, but successfully as well. He has treated not only my moods but even my fancies with the greatest consideration. . . . He cannot take away the weariness of mind which at the end of ten years of strain has come upon me; but he has done his utmost to help me to overcome it by relieving the immediate material pressure. . . . How much can he expect in return for these services? I don't know. But I fear I am not a 'profitable' man for anybody's speculation.

The breach that Pinker filled amounted at one time or another to £1,600 in advances to Conrad, and included managing Conrad's finances, down to paying for milk and cigars. In 1916 Conrad summed up Pinker's usefulness to him in a letter to John Quinn, saying that his books 'owe their existence to Mr. Pinker as much as to me'. The two men had become intimate friends by that time, and Pinker and his wife were frequent guests of the Conrads. Mrs. Conrad has described an evening when the Pinkers visited them in Corsica in 1921.

Mr. Pinker had a knack of soothing my husband in difficult moods, who needed either sympathetic indulgence or tolerant disregard. Mr. Pinker's wonderful voice was a joy and a delight to us all, and his daughter was a very able accompanist. . . .

One night my husband retired early from the dining-room, displeased with something on the menu, and we five sat laughing and talking over the rest of the meal. . . . At last no reasonable pretence remained for lingering where we were, and we prepared to return to the sitting-room at the very end of the long passage. . . . J. B. Pinker walked first, the flickering light from his candle falling on his white head. His wonderful voice rose in a sacred chant and the waiters—all Swiss—fell into line with clasped hands or making the sign of the cross. Very profane, no doubt, but inexpressibly funny because it was a sudden impulse. . . .

Mr. Pinker, deadly serious and filling the place with his voice, proceeded right to the door of our private sitting-room. Suddenly my husband flung it open and said icily: 'Yes, and I'm a Catholic, aren't I?'

. . . I passed on to my room without facing my lord and master, and left J. B. Pinker to weather the storm. For some time no sound broke the silence in the next room, then I heard the singer's voice murmuring insinuatingly, I could not catch what was said, but the effect was a peal of amused laughter from the 'Catholic' and I knew the storm was over.

Slightly more than a year later, Pinker died suddenly while on a trip to New York, and Conrad wrote to a friend: 'I have suffered a most painful loss in my old friend J. B. Pinker who died five days ago. . . . Our friendship lasted for 22 years. He was 6 years younger than myself and I feel quite overpowered by this blow of fate.'

Pinker's relationship with Bennett was rather more formal than that with Conrad, but it had the special merit of being recorded in a few thousand business letters between the two men from 1901 to 1922. Bennett came to Pinker at the behest of H. G. Wells, who was a neighbour of Pinker's in Worcester Park as well as a client; and he never had the trouble with him that he had with W. M. Colles earlier. No doubt Pinker was fortunate in that he took Bennett on just at the time when Bennett was finishing his writing apprenticeship. In any event, the next twenty years show Bennett's rise, under Pinker's guidance, from £2. 10s. per thousand words to £100 and more. 'Kindly tell me whether I ought to accept this [£2. 10s. from

Lever Tillotson],' Bennett writes to Pinker in 1903, 'as of course I shall not act contrary to your opinion. He *might* be screwed up a little more, but I doubt it.' And then in 1920, when he is dealing with Jesse Lasky (head of Famous Players Lasky, which later became Paramount Pictures): 'I expect I shall fix the main points of the contract with him personally, but of course I shall tell him that the contract must be settled between you and his representatives in London. In the meantime I should like to know from you what is the lowest advance and the lowest total figure which I ought to accept.' On this occasion Bennett accepted a figure lower than his customary rates at the time, because he was exploring the new field of film scenarios, and in the event he was paid £1,000 in advance and failed to earn the remainder, his scenario not proving acceptable.

Pinker and Bennett faced occasional troubles together. When Bennett was in America in 1911 he talked with Robert Davis of the Munsey Syndicate about serializing one or more future novels in *Munsey's Magazine*, and the discussion continued by letter on Bennett's return to England. In 1914, when Pinker himself was in America, he closed with Davis for serial publication of three novels, the first at a price of £3,000, the others for £3,500 each. These were Bennett's best contracts up to that time. The first novel, *These Twain*, was duly published and paid for, but Munsey delayed in making a deposit prior to delivery of the manuscript of the second novel, and the firm was actually trying to re-sell the contract, a fact known to Pinker. When the second novel was delivered, Davis wrote to Pinker: 'We are somewhat surprised at the receipt of *The Roll-Call*, the fourth segment in the Clayhanger series. It was understood between Arnold Bennett and myself that something in the vein of *Buried Alive* [a humorous novel] would follow.' Pinker consulted Bennett, who recalled clearly that his conversations and letters implied no such thing, and the two men realized that the Syndicate was trying one more means of getting out of the contract. Bennett proposed legal action, and Pinker agreed, saying that he had 'never suspected Davis of honesty, but I thought he would have been more skilful than he appears'. George Doran, Bennett's regular American publisher, became a reluctant intermediary. He was a friend of both Davis and Bennett, and wrote to Pinker in the midst of the quarrel:

'I am unwilling to enter into the fight, still I am not willing to shirk the slightest part of the obligations and privileges of friendship: so command me in any way you choose.' He conveyed to the Syndicate the intentions of Bennett and Pinker to sue, and obtained an offer of $10,000 (£2,000) for release from the contracts for the second and third books. Otherwise the Syndicate would fight it out in court. Doran also saw in the offices of the Syndicate a letter from Bennett to Davis in which Bennett described the second novel precisely in Davis's terms and further asserted that the fourth Clayhanger novel would not be any part of the bargain. He cabled the relevant portion of the letter to England. Bennett wrote laconically to Pinker: 'My letter to Davis seems rather categoric.' Pinker could hardly have been amused. He and Bennett agreed to accept the $10,000, and upon receipt of the sum he wrote to Bennett: 'I need not say that I am very glad this has come off. In the face of your warning of your dislike for litigation I did not like running the risk, but I had either to accept Munsey's offer or face that risk.'

On other occasions the two men did not pretend to think as one. When Bennett first went to Pinker, he brought with him the manuscript of *Anna of the Five Towns*, his first extended study of the Potteries and his first major accomplishment. W. M. Colles had not succeeded in selling it, Pinker himself was unenthusiastic, and the publisher who did take it for America, S. S. McClure, had second thoughts. Some months later, Bennett had the pleasure of writing to Pinker:

Do not fail to get the Literary Supplement to the *New York Times* for Oct 4th & see W. L. Alden's extraordinary appreciation of *Anna*. He says it is the best novel of the sort since *Esther Waters*. (It is.) You should lay it before McClures with your compliments & mine.

During the next years a more serious problem arose over Bennett's rate of work. He was producing books faster than Pinker thought advisable, and Pinker suggested holding up on certain work and not publishing in volume form the series of essays that were the start of Bennett's pocket philosophies. For Bennett there could be no argument on the point.

You would be under a false impression if you imagined that I am working at pressure. I am not. I could do lots more. I have vast leisure. When

I think that I wrote the *Grand Babylon Hotel* in less than a month & that I am taking over 3 months with *Hugo*, I ask myself, Why? You don't yet realise what an engine for the production of fiction you have in me. . . . I am never content unless I am turning out the stuff. . . . You must accustom yourself to these facts & do what you can to meet them. . . .

The public & the reviewers always have given way, & always will give way, to the idiosyncrasies of an author who is strong enough to make them. The history of literature is nothing but the performance by authors of feats which the best experience had declared could not be performed. You say, & experience would perhaps support you, that the public cannot be made to buy more than an average 2 books a year by one author. I say it can, & I am as certain that I shall make it as I am certain, my dear Pinker, that I am yours always,

E. A. Bennett

You think me a blustering person, Pinker, but I am not. The truth is you twist me round your little finger.

In that year (1904) Bennett published two books, in 1905 three, in 1906 three, in 1907 four, in 1908 (the year of *The Old Wives' Tale*) five, along with a play produced.

On another issue Pinker won hands down. That was in the matter of contract between them. Bennett shared in much of the negotiating with publishers, sometimes, as with Newman Flower in later years, because he was on cordial personal and business terms with them (on one occasion he declined a 30 per cent royalty the Pinker firm had obtained from Flower on the grounds that it was too high), and other times because he alone had developed the market. The latter situation applied to most of his journalism, and Bennett saw no reason to pay Pinker 10 per cent on such work. But the contract stipulated payment, and Bennett paid. From time to time he suggested that Pinker 'should reflect upon the point in a spirit not of law but of equity', and Pinker replied on a particular case:

The amount involved is so small that one is tempted not to argue about it. I should therefore leave it to you to decide as you please but for the principle involved, which is, of course, what interests you too. You would, I know, be the first to admit that you were able to sell those articles on those terms because of my work in building up your market. If when the market is worked up an author is going to take pieces of business into his own hands he will naturally take all the easy pieces and leave the agent the difficult ones. That would be most unfair to the agent, and it would end in changing the whole relationship. As you know, it frequently happens that there is work to do for an author which involves no commission for the agent, or a commission so insignificant as to be negligible, but at the same time it is work that the author particularly wishes done. One does it with the good will and energy that one applies to the more profitable business, but only because one has towards the author the feeling of complete service. If the author is to take isolated items of his business and withhold commission, the agent is bound to react and withhold his services where they would yield no immediate commission.

Then again Bennett wrote to Pinker in 1911, when he was first beginning to make a considerable income from his writing, rising from £276 in 1909 to £16,000 in 1912:

You will remember that when I first came to you . . . I informed you with my usual confidence that I expected ultimately to make a great deal of money, & that I wanted an arrangement by which your percentage should be somewhat smaller beyond a certain sum per annum. We agreed upon terms, of which you took note but I didn't. I have completely forgotten what they were, but it appears to me that next year they are likely to become applicable.

Pinker replied:

Our arrangement was embodied in a letter from me to you, dated December 23rd 1903, and it provides for a straight 10% commission. . . . There was never any suggestion that I should have less than my usual 10% on fiction. . . .

The contract stood, and was renewed in 1913 on the same terms. What Bennett may have had in mind was an opinion he expressed in 1903 in *How to Become an Author*. He suggests there that 'when an author's income reaches two thousand a year, the agent should be willing to accept 5 per cent. on all sums exceeding two thousand; but these details are not for the aspirant'. After Pinker's death, Bennett negotiated a new contract with the elder son, Eric Pinker, that excluded journalism and that called for a commission of 5 per cent on book contracts. He wrote to Eric at the beginning of their negotiations:

This payment of commission on such work [journalism] has stuck in my throat for many years past, and as a fact I have not mentioned to you (as an honest man would) various articles upon which you are under our contract entitled to demand a commission. The system seems to me to be inexcusably unfair, especially having regard to the fact that the bulk of my journalistic work sprang from the publication in volume form of my *Evening News* articles, to which publication J. B. was strongly opposed but which I insisted on. . . .

The chief argument J. B. brought against any change in our arrangement was that unless an agent had *all* the author's business he would not take the same interest in the author's business. This argument annoys me acutely and always did. Why should he not take the same interest?

. . . My obligations to your father were very considerable, and I have always said so openly and have always done my best to get new clients for the firm. At the same time the firm has been very well rewarded for J. B.'s faith in me, and I call that account square.

Doubtless the force of J. B. Pinker's argument was most effective when J. B. Pinker himself was expressing it. Upon his death, Bennett had written to a nephew: 'Apart from the fact that he was a very old friend of mine, he had the whole of my affairs in his hands. There is *no* other really good agent in England. The difference between a good and a bad agent might mean a difference of thousands a year to me.'

Of course there is another side to Pinker's dealings with Conrad and Bennett, and it offers evidence of what publishers often complained of: that the agent destroys the personal relationship between author and publisher. In Conrad's case, Pinker was initially barred from Conrad's transactions with William and George Blackwood, and when in 1903 Pinker took over all Conrad's work, the consequence was estrangement between Conrad and the Blackwoods. The new relationship, however, proved to be more remarkable than the old one. In Bennett's case, there never developed any loyalty on Bennett's part to a publisher, except perhaps in later years to Newman Flower, and that was a special circumstance. When he was with Chatto and Windus, Bennett wrote to Pinker: 'What I want is to be published by Methuen. How soon can I get there? Chatto's list gives me appendicitis.' He went via Arthur Waugh and Chapman and Hall, who published *The Old Wives' Tale* and let it go out of print. Bennett wrote to Pinker of Waugh: 'The fact is, he is not a business man, but a second-rate artist by temperament, with his emotions undisciplined. I like him, to talk to, but on business I am sick of him. . . . When he . . . learns that we have gone to Methuens

Henrietta St. won't hold him!' And when A. M. S. Methuen mis-handled a proposal for a cheap edition of *The Old Wives' Tale*, Bennett wrote to Pinker: 'I don't mind Methuen coming up to his office only once a week, but I strongly object to his gardening leading to this sort of thing.' He left Methuen. In the end he had so many publishers that a collected edition of his writings became impossible. His loyalty was to Pinker instead; and his loyalty proved the same thing that Conrad's did: that some agents build new relationships as well as destroy old ones.

The third of the triumvirate of powerful agents in England was Curtis Brown. He was born in America in 1866, and began a journalistic career on the *Buffalo Express* in 1884. From 1894 to 1898 he was Sunday Editor of the *New York Press*. In 1898 he came to London as the representative of the *Press* and several other American newspapers, and remained their representative for twelve or more years. Shortly after his arrival, he visited John Oliver Hobbes (Pearl Theresa Craigie), who told him that she had just finished a serial story, and thought that since he knew both American and English publishers, he might be able to help her place it. She had heard of agents, and offered to pay him a 10 per cent fee. Then Egerton Castle (who was soon to marry another agent, Golding Bright) asked him for help with American publishers. And thus in 1899 he found himself in business as head of the International Publishing Bureau at 5 Henrietta Street, Covent Garden. By about 1905 he was operating under his own name at the same address, and establishing himself as a formidable rival to Pinker and Watt. Four years later, Pinker said of him in a letter to Arnold Bennett:

Yes, I think Curtis Brown is losing ground. I like him personally, and think he is an honest, capable man, but he is like all Americans and wants to make a lot of money in a very little time. I could always see that he thought my English way was slow and rather stupid, and I do not think he ever realised that the capacity for snapping up commissions does not make a Literary Agent. . . .

Brown survived and surpassed both Pinker and Watt. His firm today, headed by his son, Spencer Curtis Brown, is the foremost international agency.

Aside from theatrical agents, the first important dramatic agent in England was Arthur Addison Bright, older brother of Golding Bright, who eventually took over part of the firm. Although little information on him survives, he seems to have been a fairly considerable person in his day. At one time or another he was dramatic critic for a London daily newspaper, and he was probably in business as an agent by the late eighties. He served J. M. Barrie, Stephen Phillips, and Sir Arthur Conan Doyle. He seems to have done some of the preliminary writing in the dramatization of *The Little Minister*. When he died, a suicide, in 1906 at the age of forty-five, he was eulogized in *The Times* by Barrie:

To the many to whom the keenly intellectual face and noble character of Arthur Addison Bright were incentives to well-doing, it will come with a painful shock that he died suddenly on Tuesday night at Lucerne. . . . Mr. Bright had for a long time represented a number of authors besides myself in their affairs of the theatre, and it was owing to his encouragement and zealous help more than to any other cause that novelists and poets have of late years produced plays. He was a man of a mind the most catholic and cultured, and of so beautiful and modest a nature that it may be said of him, he had never time to be much interested in himself he was so interested in his friends. For many years he was my most loved friend.

A short time before he wrote this, Barrie learned privately that Bright had defrauded him of £16,000, and defrauded other clients of similar sums.

VI Agency in America: Newspaper Agencies, Societies for Authors, Marbury and Reynolds

> The idea of authorship and poverty are so immediately connected, that after a man has once read Locke, and understood him, they are ever after looked upon as a part of the same complex idea of mixed modes. . . . And, first, though it frequently happens among the brethren of the quill, that many are *starved into writing*, I believe it will be found upon examination that full as many are *starved out of it*: for what with the tyranny of patentees and booksellers, the additional taxes upon paper and publication, and the little attention of the town to works of *genius*, not to say merit, it is fifty to one . . . that he does not go nine months with an empty belly, before he sells out of the bank of Parnassus, and leaves the Muses to starve by themselves.
>
> —John Atall?, *The Adventures of an Author*, 1767

The advance of authorship proceeded more slowly in America than in England. There was less to advance, despite the accomplishments of Hawthorne, Melville, Whitman, Twain, and others, and the vast unsettled state of the nation itself was a formidable barrier to the initial development of authors' organizations and literary agency. The situation was otherwise with newspaper agencies, which came into being at about the same time as in England. Elmo Scott Watson's *History of Newspaper Syndicates in America* describes a few isolated examples of syndicated news before the Civil War, going back to 1841, when Moses Beach, owner and publisher of the *New York Sun*, arranged to have a special messenger bring President Tyler's annual message to Congress to New York, where he printed it and sold copies to near-by editors for them to insert in their newspapers. With the war and the call for volunteers arose a situation that virtually necessitated syndication if rural newspapers were to survive. The editor of one such paper, Ansel Nash Kellogg of the *Baraboo Republic* (Wisconsin), found himself without the services of some of his editorial and printing staff, and he solved his problem by buying half-sheets of war news from the *Wisconsin State Journal* (a daily) to fold within his own half-sheets. Later he bought full sheets printed on one side, and filled the other side himself. Other rural Wisconsin papers followed suit, likewise buying from the *Journal*, and the latter paper soon had a profitable enterprise supplying about thirty weeklies with such sheets.

67

Kellogg saw a future in what he had indirectly started, and in 1865 he sold his paper and went to Chicago to set up in business as a supplier of inside sheets to rural newspapers. The return of the veterans did not at all spoil his prospects, and within months he was thriving. His material at first consisted of miscellaneous small items and a story. Whether the story was fiction or an account of someone's adventures in the frozen North is not clear. By 1867 he was providing political material to suit the taste of individual newspapers (performing what a later age would call a personalized service), and by 1875, if not earlier, he and others were supplying serial fiction. By the time he died in 1886 he was reportedly supplying nearly 1,400 rural papers with his sheets. He had competitors from the very start, and Watson gives the seventies as the years of the great initial flourishing of newspaper agencies. Metropolitan syndication did not begin on a large scale until the eighties, presumably because the need for outside material and outside help was less immediately pressing in the cities. S. S. McClure, perhaps the most famous of the newspaper agents in America, started his business on a shoestring in 1884, and very soon was the master of an empire. He specialized in fiction, and went to England to talk high prices with A. P. Watt and the Tillotsons for English literary lions. Two of his offers to Robert Louis Stevenson are noted on page 88.

The struggle to improve the condition of authorship was all but won, as far as it could be won, before American authors got around to organizing themselves to secure that improvement. The first considerable attempt of this sort seems to have been the Association of American Authors, founded in New York City in 1892. The immediate inspiration for organization came from an article by George Haven Putnam in *Forum* in September 1891. Despite a sympathy for authors that set him apart from some of his fellow publishers, Putnam consented to be the villain here. He argued that the numerous complaints of authors indicated that something was wrong, but he was inclined to think that authors were born complainers and that by and large publishers were honest and fairminded. Among the readers of the article was Charles Burr Todd, author of books on the real Aaron Burr and the real Benedict Arnold. He decided to make an auctorial complaint, and first he got in touch with Sir Walter Besant and then he approached Walter Hines Page, editor of *Forum* and a man who evidently had some interest in the welfare of authors (see page 81). Page agreed that Besant and Todd should respond to Putnam, and they did so in the issue of the following March, Besant with an account of the Society of Authors and Todd with a separate article arguing the plight of the American author. Among other things Todd's article says that Putnam's claim that the accounts of publishers are open to inspection is untrue. The author who asks to see his publisher's accounts is not likely to have the same publisher for his next book. At the end of the article Todd recommends the forming of an American society of authors.

In the very same month, Todd and some other writers gathered in New York City to form such a society. The invitation to the meeting was signed by W. D. Howells, George W. Cable, Thomas D. Higginson, and Moncure Conway (whose activities as an informal literary agent are noted on page 31) among others. Todd himself was the prime mover. Shortly before the meeting he received a disgruntled communication from an already existing and obscure Society of American Authors, and at the meeting itself members of the other Society caused some dissension. Already W. D. Howells had backed out because he had not wanted his name used publicly; and the venture threatened to sink before it was launched. But it did survive, and lasted ten years. Higginson was the first President, Conway was one of the Vice-Presidents, and Todd was Secretary. The activities of the Association (later called the American Authors' Guild) included publishing a *Bulletin* and a brochure on publishing costs, arbitrating author–publisher disputes, and providing funds for aged or indigent members. The organization held monthly receptions, and on one occasion fêted Mark Twain. It was this activity, says Todd in his account of the Association, that was their downfall. They were more social than political and literary.

The Authors' League of America, the major organization of American authors to this day, came into existence in 1912, and according to one of its founders, Arthur Train (lawyer and creator of the legal figure Mr. Tutt, who entertained many an immature mind in the earlier decades of this century), the inspiration for the

founding was again of an immediate sort—the Dam *v.* Kirk La
Shelle Company decision by the U. S. Circuit Court of Appeals,
Second Circuit, in January 1910. In 1901 Henry J. W. Dam sold a
story to *Smart Set*, with no stipulation with regard to copyright by
either side. (The general assumption at the time was apparently that
in such a sale all that was sold were serial rights.) *Smart Set* published the story along with a notice of copyright. Later another
author based a play on the story, and the Kirk La Shelle Company
produced it. Dam sued, alleging at first that he had parted only
with his serial rights to *Smart Set* and retained all other rights, and
then alleging that he had sold all rights. La Shelle argued that since
Dam hadn't parted with all rights, the dramatic rights were in fact
unprotected. But the Court found that such a sale as Dam had made
did involve all rights, and thus that La Shelle had infringed the
copyright of *Smart Set*. The Court went on to say that had Dam
meant to offer only serial rights, the copyright by *Smart Set* would
presumably have been meant to cover only serial rights, and the
dramatic rights would then have been unprotected unless Dam
copyrighted them himself. The decision, says Train, threatened
authors with a total loss of copyright; and the Authors' League was
founded to save the day. And the day was saved, though not by
overthrowing the decision.

On the Council of the Authors' League in its first year were Train,
Gertrude Atherton, Hamlin Garland, Ellen Glasgow, Ida Tarbell,
and others. In a pamphlet issued by the League in that year the
purposes of the League are set forth: improvement of domestic and
international copyright legislation; protection of the rights and
properties of authors; assistance to authors in disposing of their
properties and in securing their legal rights; and provision of a
reading bureau to advise young authors (at the rate of $5.00 for
stories up to 7,000 words and $10.00 for novels up to 100,000).
'The writer', says the pamphlet, 'owing to his temperament, his lack
of business training, and his frequent isolation from other members
of his profession, is especially unfitted to drive a good bargain with
those who buy his manuscripts.' Beginning in the following year,
the League issued a *Bulletin*, which had the same function as the
Author in England but which proved to be a tame affair. It had a

complaints department and reported on new copyright legislation and the like, but the tone was never militant, and in due course there appeared a series of articles on 'Our Friends the Editors'. Much space was given to descriptions of journalistic markets. There was never any broad attack on either publishers or agents, and one of the few discussions of the agent question justified the charging of reading fees by the agent on the ground that it discouraged the tyro from plaguing the agent with all his unpublishable work. To the Society of Authors the reading fee was the obvious mark of dishonesty.[1]

Sixteen years after the founding of the League, Train, who was then President, summed up its activities and to him the record was impressive. In that time membership had advanced from 350, as of April 1913, to 2,094; the League had been mightily instrumental in securing equitable treatment of authors by publishers; and the League had rendered considerable financial assistance to unfortunate authors and their families. In the past year, said Train, the League revised 35 book contracts for members, read and filed 320 play contracts, collected royalties in the amount of $54,000, disbursed $9,000 to 30 writers in distress (16 male and 14 female). Moreover, 1,708 people called at the office; 31,446 pieces of mail were sent out, 5,000 of them individually dictated (the round figure here is inexplicable); and 16,375 telephone calls were made. In view of this success, said Train, it was time for the League to do something to advance the spiritual state of American literature, and he suggested the giving of an annual prize.

The function of the League as a literary agent seems to have been even less effective than that of the Society of Authors. There were

1 The difference of attitude here perhaps simply reflects a difference of condition. To this day the *Writer* and the *Writer's Digest*, the best journals of their sort in America, contain many advertisements by apparently reputable people who are willing to consult with young authors for a price. Their activity is by and large quite distinct from that of the New York agents. Such advisers are conducting creative and commercial writing courses for people who study mainly at home. Similar activity seems to exist on a far smaller scale in England, and has perhaps always been less reputable and less naïve. The characteristic English scorn for university courses in writing seems of the same piece. The two nations take different attitudes towards the business and art of writing—the one a nation in which a subtle sense of language and culture is evident at all levels of society, the other a nation that is still trying by conscious means to acquire both language and culture.

at least three good reasons: (1) the League came into being when the private agents were much more firmly entrenched; (2) the League made no serious effort to compete with private agents in knowledge of the market; (3) the League wanted a 10 per cent commission too. In 1912 there were a dozen or more competent private agents on the scene, operating individually or soon to do so, among them Elisabeth Marbury, Paul Reynolds, Harold Ober, Ann Watkins, Nannine Joseph, and Alice Kauser. The leading English agents —Watt, Pinker, and Brown—either had their own offices in New York or connections with one of the New York agents.

The origins of the American agents are of the same ambiguous and accidental sort as the English, and their emergence coincides with other activity on the author's behalf. In 1878 there existed at 252 Broadway an Athenaeum Bureau of Literature, which invited correspondence from authors wishing to sell manuscripts. In 1882 or 1883 there came into being the New York Bureau of Literary Revision, which lasted at least nine years and drew some not unfavourable attention from Sir Walter Besant. And in 1887 the *Writer*, the most reputable journal of its sort in America, was founded, and in its first year instituted a Writer's Literary Bureau, which undertook to advise authors and correct manuscripts for a small fee. It is not clear whether the Bureau forwarded manuscripts to publishers. In 1891 William H. Hills, editor and publisher of the journal, explained 'the usefulness of . . . a well-conducted literary bureau': to sift the chaff from the wheat and so help aspiring authors and also editors and publishers. The *Ladies' Home Journal*, he said, received 15,000 manuscripts the previous year; it accepted 497, of which only 197 were unsolicited by the editors themselves. Why should the operation be so inefficient, and why should obscure authors have the smaller slice of the cake?

The first notable agent on the American scene—apart from such figures as Conway—seems to have been Elisabeth Marbury, who also has the distinction of being the only early agent to write a substantial account of her career, in *My Crystal Ball*. She was born of a well-to-do family in New York in 1856. Her father, who was a lawyer, was a friend of James Russell Lowell; and at home and on trips to England, where Lowell was for a time ambassador, Miss

Marbury met many notable men of the day, including Darwin, Huxley, and Spencer. In 1885 or 1886, while she was preparing a benefit performance of a play, she met Daniel Frohman, who suggested to her that she had good business sense and ought to do something with it. Soon thereafter she learned that Mrs. Frances Hodgson Burnett was to have *Little Lord Fauntleroy* produced on Broadway and needed a representative to conduct negotiations and attend rehearsals. She arranged an introduction, became the representative, and when the play proved successful, continued as Mrs. Burnett's personal agent in all her literary affairs. This work went on for several years. Then during a trip to Paris she lost a considerable sum of money. She decided to meet the crisis by becoming an agent for the sale of French plays in America. Up to that time French plays were sold outright for a small fixed sum for American performance; and she thought of introducing a royalty system so that the author would benefit proportionately if the play was a success. She took her idea to Victorien Sardou, President of the Société des Gens de Lettres, and won his approval. Within a short time she became the official agent for most of the French dramatists for the sale of their works in all English-speaking countries. Soon afterwards she established a New York office, and later had offices in London (in association with Addison Bright and then Golding Bright), Madrid, Milan, and Berlin. Most of her important American and English clients were dramatists: Clyde Fitch, Oscar Wilde, Bernard Shaw; but she also handled novelists, among them Owen Johnson, whose most famous work, *Stover at Yale*, has survived his name. One of her employees was Alice Kauser, who later started a successful independent agency. Miss Marbury's activities as an agent were often secondary to other interests, personal and social. After 1918 she was prominent in the Democratic party in New York. Her death in 1933 elicited a public tribute from President-elect Roosevelt, but none from any writers.

The most important early agent in America was Paul Revere Reynolds, an account of whom was written by Frederick Lewis Allen. He was born in Boston in 1864. His grandfather was a noted physician; his uncle was Wendell Phillips. He went to Harvard to study literature and philosophy, took a job briefly with the publisher

6

Lothrop in Boston, returned to Harvard for a Master's degree, and then with the help of his friend Mark DeWolfe Howe became a reader for *Youth's Companion*. In 1891 he gave up Boston to try New York, and began to make his way there as a reviewer for such publications as the *Episcopal Churchman*. By chance he fell in with O. M. Dunham, a sometime newspaper proprietor, who was the New York representative for Cassells. Dunham's task was to publish such Cassell books as he thought would sell in America, and he was doing the job none too satisfactorily. Cassells thought that other publishers might be interested in books that he rejected, and asked whether he knew anyone who could show the books around. He suggested Reynolds, and thus Reynolds was launched as a publisher's agent. Within about a year he fairly well usurped Dunham's position. In a letter from Cassells of 20 July 1892 it was agreed that he would be their New York representative for the sum of $500 per annum. His duties were (1) to give Dunham the first refusal on any Cassell book and then try to sell it elsewhere, (2) to advise Cassells on new American books that might be of interest to them, (3) to assist in any other negotiations they undertook with an American author or publisher, and (4) to do anything else he pleased except become a similar agent for another firm. This contract continued until 1898, when he and Cassells parted over a disagreement on terms. Item 4 was abrogated within a year. In June 1893 William Heinemann was in New York and asked Reynolds to be his agent, apparently untroubled by any thought that a publisher's agent might be just as unsubstantial a fellow as an author's agent and might even transform himself into one. The arrangement was made with Cassells's blessing. A few months later Reynolds also became agent for Sampson, Low, and Marston, and somewhat later for Constable. More important, he began now to make direct approaches to American authors to publish with Cassells; and by 1895 he was acting for authors independently, carrying their wares to a variety of publishers and charging them 10 per cent on sales for his work. His clients included Stephen Crane, Ellen Glasgow, Paul Lawrence Dunbar, and many of the most famous English writers of the day.

The particular interest of Reynolds's career is that in a much more conspicuous way than his fellows he was a double agent, serving both publishers and authors. Some agents, notably J. B. Pinker, were quite certain that a good agent could and ought to have only one master; and the threat of the double agent was time and again remarked upon in the public discussion of literary agency in its early days. But there is no evidence to suggest that Reynolds used his position dishonestly, and his situation mainly illustrates that both the origin and destiny of literary agency could hardly help being impure. Men became agents in accidental ways; and whether formally or informally, agents today act for publishers perhaps as much as for authors. It is clear that at least until 1904 Reynolds made his living chiefly as an agent for English publishers and English authors (serving the latter largely through connections with Pinker, Curtis Brown, and the Literary Agency of London). Afterwards he began to shift his attention from books to serial publication, and here too he was in effect a double agent. The *Saturday Evening Post*, whose circulation rose from the hundred thousands in the nineties to two million in 1914 and three million in 1927, became his chief outlet for material. Once a week a *Post* representative called on him. It is hard to imagine that the two men were unaware of how useful they were to each other. Nevertheless, the *Post* saw fit to raise its rates for a story from a top rate of $400 to $2,000 and more during this period, so that authors benefited too. In 1905 Reynolds took into his office Harold Ober, who later began a successful agency of his own. Reynolds chose to keep his business small and uncompartmentalized. He had no contracts with his authors. They were free to break off as they wished. They were also free to write him frantic letters asking for money. Thus Stephen Crane, writing from Cuba: 'For Christ's sake get me some money quick here by cable.' Paul Lawrence Dunbar wrote similar, more polite letters. Reynolds seems to have responded generously to such pleas, and he had his reward. He was active up to his death in 1944, and left a thriving business to his son.

VII Three-Cornered Quarrel: Agency until the Forties

Booksellers . . . it seems, claim an equal privilege with the rest of their fellow citizens engaged in trade, to eat and drink; and if in the good graces of dame Fortune, to leave estates to their families. But authors, it seems, are beings of a very high order, and infinitely above the low considerations of the useful, the convenient, and the necessary!
—Catherine Macaulay, *A Modest Plea For the Property of Copyright*, 1774

Anyone who read the *Publishers' Circular* in the latter part of the nineteenth century would have seen the editors in training for a quarrel with the agents. In 1859 they take James Lowe to task for accusing publishers of occasional sharp practice with authors: preposterous, they say, at least with any publisher who values his name. In 1863 and again in 1864 they attack a magazine that an author has called a 'literary court of conscience'—doubtless the *Athenaeum*. Why does the magazine see fit to print authors' complaints against publishers? Would *The Times* print a complaint of a man against a contractor who had not built his house properly? In 1865 they think that in these days of life insurance there is no need for other organizations to assist writers in distress. In 1871 they observe that 'the world is well disposed to its authors, notwithstanding on their part a certain quarrelsomeness, self-assertion, and petulance, which is inseparable from the race'. The following year Longmans publish a book on copyright, in which authors are warned never to surrender their copyrights; and the editors remind Longmans that the interests of author and publisher are identical. So things go, year after year. When two young publishing houses collapse, the editors reflect that writers ought to be grateful for the existence of old-established firms. On another occasion they admit that writers do not make fortunes, but think that being able to earn money on one's own is compensation. Shortly thereafter they assure writers that the several thousand pounds paid for *Daniel Deronda* does not at all mean that writing pays well. When Frederick Macmillan calls the supposed antagonism between author and publisher 'a foolish and mischievous fancy', they lay the blame upon foolish authors. It is surprising, then, that in all these years, from 1859 to 1892, when they comment on Macmillan's words, there appears to be hardly a reference to literary agency in the *Circular*. Apparently the agents were so few in number, so contemptible, or (like Watt for a time) so discreet and serviceable, that the danger went unmentioned.

Doubtless the publishers were aware of trouble. In 1887 the Society of Authors sponsored three talks (collected under the title *The Grievances Between Authors and Publishers*) in which Walter Besant and others accused the publishers of selfishness and dishonesty in their dealings with authors. Besant looked forward to the day when the Society of Authors would be a gigantic publishing house in which authors took their own risks and won all the rewards. A few of the publishers wrote aggrieved letters to *The Times*; Smith, Elder were certain that to some authors 'a chance of imprisoning . . . publishers would be . . . a vision of delight'. In the next two years the Society published *The Cost of Publishing* and *Methods of Publishing*, which were designed as aids to the author in negotiating contracts, and which elicited from one eminent author the view that he would rather be cheated than do arithmetic. In these same years *Tit-Bits* entertained its readers with tales of bogus publishers ('Confessions of a Publisher's Reader' and the like). And Cassells had the misfortune to make a huge profit out of Dean Farrar's *Life of Christ*, reportedly £50,000 to Farrar's £2,000, and the scandal went round the world. A writer named Augustus Jessop made 'A Plea for the Publisher' in the *Contemporary Review* in 1890, saying how excellently he had always been treated by them; and Andrew Lang averred in the *St. James's Gazette* that he was quite content for publishers to get the better of him occasionally. But such comments were unconvincing. In 1892 the publishers made their own attack. On 3 December in the *Athenaeum* William Heinemann described the Society of Authors as 'a trades union more complete, more dangerous . . . more determined in its demands than any of the other unions—conducted, besides, with intelligence, with foresight, with purity of purpose, but unquestionably and avowedly against the publisher'. He went on to recommend the forming of a publishers' union. The essay drew comment in the *Athenaeum* and half a dozen other papers for the next two months. On the publishers' side, George Bentley, John Murray, and others came in to describe the risks of publishing and to challenge the figures of the Society of Authors on the costs of publishing. Murray cited good books that had lost £1,729 and £2,311 for their publisher. Heinemann argued that the publishers' profits calculated by the Society neglected to account for working costs. Someone else wanted to know who the members of the Society were, and thought that the publishers could do without their services. (George Meredith was then President of the Society.) Walter Besant did most of the counter-attacking. Little was said of literary agency except for George Bentley's remark that the agent's fee really came from the pocket of the publisher. Later in 1893 most of the exchanges were gathered without comment into a volume entitled *The Hardships of Publishing*, which was printed privately by the Ballantyne Press. Heinemann sponsored the book, apparently believing—rightly it seems—that the publishers had the better of Besant in the argument; and it includes some private correspondence between Heinemann and other publishers about the publishers' union.[1] The epigraph of the book is the fable of the man who killed the goose that laid the golden egg. Only one notable exchange is omitted from the book. On 21 January 1893 in the *Athenaeum* Heinemann had quoted a letter from Rudyard Kipling in which Kipling thanked him for his essay of 3 December and said that authors were too ready to call publishers Barabbas. On 18 February Kipling wrote in to say that his letter to Heinemann had been a civil private letter, not intended for publication. Otherwise he would have had more to say. 'My practice', he concluded, '(for I have bought my experience in the market) is to deal with publishers entirely through an agent.'

The quarrel was now open and general. On a trip to America Besant delivered an unusually harsh attack on the publishers, accusing them of widespread fraud under the half-profit system and anticipating nothing better under the royalty system unless publishers' accounts were regularly opened to audit. The *Author*

---

1 The Publishers' Association, founded in 1895, came into existence mainly as a result of the quarrel about the overpricing of books. See Sir Frederick Macmillan, *The Net Book Agreement, 1899*, 1924. What influence the present quarrel had on the forming of the Association is not known.

printed the address in September 1893. That November Heinemann made his attack on A. P. Watt, who was Kipling's agent. For the next several years the publishers and Besant continued to argue publicly about publishing costs. The chief outside supporter of the publishers during these years was Andrew Lang. He hated to think that authors were such miserable weak creatures that they could not take care of themselves, and at the same time he knew only one of them, the poet Collins, who had ever returned money to a publisher who had lost on a book. He found the tales of woe in the *Author* fanciful and entertaining. Edmund Gosse attacked authors for their 'unbridled greed', apparently with Hall Caine especially in mind— and Gosse on the one hand was a member of the Council of the Society of Authors and a contributor to *The Grievances Between Authors and Publishers* and on the other hand literary adviser to Heinemann, who happened to be Hall Caine's publisher. From across the Atlantic William Dean Howells wished 'to bear my witness to the constant good faith and uprightness of publishers'. For their part, a few of the publishers defended the authors. One of the most notable among them was another American, George Haven Putnam, who in an article in *Forum* in 1891 asserted the right of authors to know the publishing statistics on their books without having to ask for them. Putnam was the author of *Authors and Publishers*, first published in 1883, a book which, while it took conventional views about the interests of authors and publishers being identical, displayed a general sympathy for the situation of the author. The seventh edition, of 1897, offered perhaps the first formal expression of approval of the literary agent by a publisher. On the English side, two early sympathizers were Andrew Tuer and Andrew Chatto, Sr. In 1883 it was rumoured that a book was being written on the quarrel between authors and publishers, and the editors of the *Athenaeum* doubted that a publisher would risk offending his brothers by publishing it. Tuer came forward to say that he had commissioned the book, 'to lay bare the grisly secrets of the quarrel', but that the writer had been unable to do the work. Tuer was later a contributor to and the publisher of *The Grievances Between Authors and Publishers*. Andrew Chatto's letter to Watt in Watt's first collection of letters was the only one from a publisher that was explicit and generous. The letter was dated 1885. In the nineties or earlier he was recommending to writers that they employ Watt.

The quarrel over literary agency itself was conducted sporadically, and the Society of Authors battled against the agents more openly than did the publishers. With the publishers the argument took mainly the view that the agents interfered with the right relationship between author and publisher and that they debased literature by emphasizing the commercial aspect. From the nineties until his death in 1920 William Heinemann was the chief spokesman for this view. In 1901 the *Author* very kindly opened its pages to him to explain why the agents served neither publisher nor author nor literature:

1. *The Publisher.*—(*a*) Because the literary agent prevents that free and intimate intercourse between author and publisher which is from my experience of unquestioned mutual advantage.

(*b*) Because I have not found literary agents scrupulously honest in their dealings.

(*c*) Because I resent the implied imputation that the publisher might take advantage of an author. . . .

(*d*) Because I do not consider it in the interest of *my* individual business or in the interests of publishers in general that one of us should be played off against the other, as is the habit and practically the *raison d'être* of the literary agent.

(*e*) Because no author would be so quixotic as to employ a literary agent if he did not hope to get as much more out of the publisher as the agent's commission represents.

2. *The Author.*—(*a*) Because I believe it to be in many instances of advantage to authors to be in personal communication with their publishers.

(*b*) Because I consider it *infra dignitatem auctoris* to assume that he cannot take care of himself should he really come into contact with an overreaching publisher. . . .

(*c*) Because the author's agent is successful only after an author's reputation has been established by the publisher, but never with a young and unknown writer, so that he merely comes in for an enormous share of profits. . . .

(*d*) Because the author's agent fosters in authors the greed for an immediate money return . . . at the cost of all dignity and artistic repose. . . .

3. *Literature.*—(*a*) Because I do not consider it to be in the interests of literature that books should be put up to auction. . . .

(*b*) Because it is certainly very much against the interests of literature that authors should be pledged and sold body and soul to syndicates and publishers. . . .

(*c*) Because of the fact that it discourages the publisher from taking up new authors, if they are, as soon as he has borne the first risk and launched them, to be put up to public auction. . . .

Other publishers usually took the same high tone as Heinemann, though occasionally they struck a commercial note, as did Heinemann himself in suggesting that authors expected their 10 per cent payments to the agents to come finally from the pockets of the publishers. In 1894 an anonymous American publisher wrote to the *Athenaeum* to warn authors that agents would lead them from publisher to publisher, and thus lose for them the value of being associated with a single firm. In 1905 Walter Hines Page, of Double-day, Page, issued anonymously his *A Publisher's Confession*, in which he lamented the passing of 'that fine indifference to commercial results' which once characterized literature. Part of the blame lay with publishers themselves, but Page also attacked authors for de-manding exorbitant royalties (more than 10 per cent, except for very popular authors) and for traipsing from publisher to publisher —ending as nobody's man. His account of the production of a book described 'the divers problems which constantly arise—every step of the way beset with expense, so that the publisher is amazed when he finds a surplus'. He did not mention literary agency, and else-where he spoke favourably of the profession, but his book elicited a long essay on 'The Commercialization of Literature' from Henry Holt in the *Atlantic*, November 1905, in which the ills of exorbi-tant royalties and inconstancy were attributed to the agents. Holt acknowledged that agents sometimes performed useful services, but he thought that any competent publisher could do better. Agents lured authors with the promise of El Dorado, but were proving to be 'a very serious detriment to literature and a leech on the author'. Agency was already declining.

Earlier in the year, William Swan Sonnenschein, the head of Routledge, made an attack on agents in an interview in *Publisher and Bookseller*, a short-lived journal whose editors were sympathetic to agents. He thought that the best service of the agent was in accountancy, for which a professional fee should be paid. Otherwise the agent was useless, and in fact was in decline. Curiously enough, Routledge took over the publication of the *Literary Year-Book* in 1905, and Sonnenschein could have found evidence in it of a steady rise in the importance of literary agency over the eight years in which the *Year-Book* had been issued: a phrase alluding to agency the first year; a footnote the second year, in which Watt and Colles were mentioned; a formal list of eight agents the third year; and fourteen English agents, four American, and several special agents by 1905. Less curiously, there appeared in the *Year-Book* for the first time in 1905 an anonymous attack on agents. Said the author: If in the past the publisher had his own interest uppermost, today he was forced even further in the same direction by the agents. Writers should never bind themselves to agents for future books, and they should never pay a percentage on royalties. They should realize, the author said incidentally, that an advance against royalties was tantamount to borrowing.

The case against the agent was none too easy for the publisher to document in public, and in fact much of the argument both for and against was conducted abstractly. One publisher, Sir Stanley Unwin, made harsh generalizations about agency and was taken to task for it, and some years later he made the same remarks again, noting that in the meantime three agents had been convicted of dishonesty. William Heinemann documented his case in 1918. In November of that year he sent to the *Publishers' Circular* a copy of a letter that had been mailed to several of his young authors by Watt. In the letter the late W. P. Watt said that he had been asked by an excellent and enterprising publisher if the author in question would be interested in placing his next work with that publisher. Should the author allow Watt to act as his agent, there was no doubt that good terms could be arranged. Heinemann told the *Publishers' Circular* that he was flattered at the thought of another publisher wanting his list. Such an enterprising publisher too: ready to save himself the endless trouble of developing his own list. And as for Watt, 'that versatile gentleman' was now a publisher's agent as well as an author's agent. In one or another version of Watt's letter, the author was guaranteed that the enterprising publisher would take up to three novels, sight unseen. Such faith in my judgement! said Heinemann. All the letters were sent to the authors care of Heinemann, who forwarded them unopened, and learned their contents from the authors. The response to Heinemann's revelation was silence by Watt and applause by John Murray, Sir Stanley Unwin, and Edmund Gosse. A translator, Fitzwater Wray, wrote in to say that he had received a similar letter in 1917, and the agent had lost interest in him as soon as it appeared that he did not own the copyright of material he was presumed to own. An anonymous 'Reader' came to Watt's defence, arguing that no publisher had a proprietary right to his authors, and that Heinemann's task was to make it unattractive for authors to want to leave him. The editors of the *Publishers' Circular* speculated that 'Reader' was a reader for an Irish publisher. Heinemann closed the correspondence by wondering why 'Reader' should be unwilling to identify himself, and thinking that he might be Watt or the enterprising publisher in disguise. A year later, not long before his death, Heinemann wrote to the *Circular* again to say that one of the young authors approached by Watt responded to his invitation and entrusted her next book to him. Heinemann assumed at the time that the book was taken by the particular enterprising publisher, but he eventually learned that this was not so. He thought that the fact revealed the true nature of Watt's letter.

The Society of Authors regarded agency in a somewhat different light from the publishers. That it was a danger there was no doubt (unless conducted by the Society of Authors, as one critic remarked); but for them the chief point was that the agents were not so much authors' agents as agents' agents and publishers' agents; and they could have offered Heinemann's experience with W. P. Watt as illustration. They were preoccupied with securing for the author the best commercial advantage, and their fundamental advice was: 'Don't employ an agent; but if you do, watch him.' Much of their comment on agency pointed out examples of fraud or questionable practice. In the early days it was thought important to warn authors against agents who charged an initial fee for reading manuscripts, such a fee being *prima facie* evidence that the agent was in business to read. They were certain that the agent could not place work which the author himself could not place, that he was of no use to beginners, and that wherever he was useful the Society of Authors could be equally useful and much less expensive. Walter Besant suggested an origin of agency that was as curious as Heinemann's: he thought they had come into existence (*a*) to protect the author from having to go to the publisher in ignorance and dependence and (*b*) to protect the publisher from being thought a screw or cheat. He hoped and expected that they would die away. When the Society faced the fact that authors would go to agents in spite of everything, they recommended (in 1912) the following agreement: a contract for twelve months, the agent to act for all rights; the agent to keep the author fully informed of his work; the agent not to enter into agreements for the author but only to submit tentative agreements; the agent to collect royalties and deduct a 10 per cent fee.

Apart from Besant, who died in 1901, the chief spokesman for most of these views was the Secretary of the Society for many years, G. Herbert Thring, whose pedestrian virtues seem to have complemented those of W. M. Colles in rendering the Society an ineffective antagonist of the private agent. The most impressive statement against the private agent to appear in the *Author* came from George Bernard Shaw, a member of the Council of the Society, in an article in 1911. Some members of the Society, says Shaw, are surprised that the Society suggests dispensing with agents. They imagine that their interests are one with those of the agent and that the publisher is the enemy. They believe the agent when the agent says that the more the author gets, the more he himself gets, implying that it behoves him to get more for them both. With a given book this may be so, since the agent gets a percentage, but in the long run things are different. The agent has to bargain with a publisher, and he soon finds out that if he is easy on the publisher he can place a dozen books at 10 or 15 per cent royalty in the time it would take to fight out one or two at 20 per cent. And if the author should realize that the royalty the agent has arranged is less than it might be, the agent has merely to say that he has only so much time to give to a book. 'Finally he settles down into an agent whose real business it is to procure books for publishers, articles for editors, and plays for managers.' To make the interests of authors and agents identical, says Shaw, the agents ought to pay their authors a percentage on the agents' annual profits from all the books they place. This is not likely to happen, and Shaw would like to see the face of the agent to whom it is proposed. Shaw does see some use for the agent. Being a powerful man with the publishers, the agent can give a quick boost to a new young writer when he wants, and very likely many young writers are glad to pay more than the normal percentage to obtain such an advantage. Then there is the great mass of hack writing, the production of which is entirely a business activity, and Shaw sees no reason why agents should not handle it. His final judgement on agents is the same as his judgement on teachers and very much like Heinemann's on A. P. Watt: 'the literary agency is a . . . favourite resort of persons who have not ability enough either for ordinary business pursuits or for literature.'

One of the more substantial documents offered by the Society of Authors in the argument against agency was published in 1937, towards the end of the open quarrel. In contrast to the Heinemann–W. P. Watt affair, this was a case of the opened letter. On 7 June 1937 the Curtis Brown agency wrote to Harper's in America, for whom Curtis Brown was the English agent, asking if the writer Leo Huberman would be interested in doing a history of America for Gollancz. (Mr. Spencer Curtis Brown tells me that Harper's were the publishers of and had controlled all rights in Huberman's books, the most recent of which Curtis Brown had sold for Harper's to Gollancz.) Harper's cabled that Huberman was interested, and supplied his English address. Curtis Brown then wrote to Huberman, saying that Harper's had indicated he was interested and explaining that they were Harper's agent. They asked him to come in and discuss the matter. The meeting took place, and the question arose as to whether Huberman should employ Curtis Brown as his agent. He decided to defer his decision until he had spoken to Victor Gollancz. When he saw Gollancz, he learned that Curtis Brown had not been instrumental in getting the offer from Gollancz but that Gollancz had written directly to him, care of Curtis Brown, whom Gollancz knew to be the English agents of Huberman's American publisher. Curtis Brown had opened the letter, and then written their own letter to Harper's. Huberman thereupon wrote to Curtis

Brown asking (1) why they had not forwarded the letter, (2) why they opened it, (3) why, once they opened it, they did not inform him of its existence and full contents, and (4) why they communicated some of the contents to a third party. Curtis Brown replied that they always attended to all business on an author's behalf so as not to trouble him unnecessarily. Huberman went to his solicitor, who suggested that the Publishers' Association or the Society of Authors should arbitrate. Curtis Brown refused to consider either possibility: they had explained themselves fully and satisfactorily. There the matter rested, so far as the *Author* was concerned. They presented the case 'without comment'.

In all the argument against agency, and in the whole quarrel between author and publisher, it is observable that official voices were not the same as private voices, and that private persons often spoke out of both sides of their mouths. Heinemann employed Paul Reynolds in New York for his own purposes, and was on friendly terms with W. M. Colles as early as 1893. Walter Besant customarily attacked the agents and employed Watt for eighteen years. Whether the *Publishers' Circular* represented the public views of publishers is uncertain, and the *Author* clearly did not express editorially the public views of many of its individual members. On more than one occasion when the *Author* attacked the agents, it received letters from members decrying its attitude. After an attack in 1911, May Sinclair wrote in to say that most of the prominent members of the Society employed agents. Of course there were dishonest agents, but she could testify for one honourable agent who occasionally acted against his own interests to serve her. As for agents taking authors from publisher to publisher, was not that a moral question for authors themselves as well as for their agents? In 1932 the *Author* made a concession in its attack by holding a symposium among a few members who favoured agency. By way of preface the editors noted that in the preceding year they had received proportionately more complaints against agents than against publishers, and they felt that the only way the agents could put their house in order was to form an association with rules and regulations about the proper conduct of business. In the symposium, Clemence Dane and Ernest Raymond spoke appreciatively of their agents, and Hugh Walpole said that J. B. Pinker had helped him so much in his early years that it would be churlish of him to say anything against the profession. If Walpole had a complaint at all, it was that the 10 per cent fee on the royalties of a given book went on year after year. Gerald Bullett had a reservation too: he thought that for serial work the agent was invaluable, but otherwise he reckoned that a well-established author would save by employing a salaried expert. And Laurence Housman described how his reservations had fallen away. Housman first went to an agent thirty years before, and explained that he needed someone to handle serial rights. He had no trouble marketing his books on his own. The agent declined the work on the grounds that serial placement was relatively difficult and unrewarding, and he needed the remuneration from easier work for the task to be worth his while. Besides, serial placements would increase the value of Housman's books, and Housman alone would get the benefit if the agent confined himself to serial work. The argument convinced Housman. But then he learned about the continuing 10 per cent deduction on his royalties, and decided that such an arrangement was intolerable. So he and the agent wrote a contract that enabled him to withdraw his work wholly and completely from the agent upon six months' notice, and recover all royalties thereafter for himself. In the event, he never saw fit to withdraw, and he did not expect to until he was tired of writing.

Most of the opponents of agency did concede a certain usefulness to the profession. If an author and his publisher were personal friends, that free and intimate intercourse between them might be abetted if someone else handled the money. One wit suggested that the author might lament with the publisher over his inability to control his agent's exorbitant demands. Or if the author was a very busy man or had no taste or talent for business, he would have reason to employ an agent. The incompetent author seemed to some people the irrefutable example to justify agency. If Heinemann wanted writers to be above commercialism, the incompetent author was just the man for him—leaving all mundane thought to an agent. No one offered Robert Louis Stevenson as the prime example on the point, but he very likely was. George L. McKay has chronicled his troubles in *Some Notes on Robert Louis Stevenson, His Finances and His*

Agents and Publishers. From the beginning of his career to the end, when his earnings were considerable, he was in financial difficulties because of generosity, carelessness, and indifference to business. From 1870 to 1887 his income from writing was not enough to support him, and in the earliest years he was sometimes near to starvation. His career was launched with the assistance of half a dozen informal agents, notably Sidney Colvin and Philip Gilbert Hammerton. Colvin met him in 1873 and almost immediately arranged for the publication of his first paid article, 'Roads', in *Portfolio*, where Colvin himself occasionally published. Colvin then wrote to the editors of *Macmillan's Magazine*, the *Cornhill*, and the *Academy*, who in due course took other pieces. Hammerton arranged for the book publication of *Notes on Edinburgh* and *Travels with a Donkey*. Eventually Stevenson's travels added another reason for needing others to handle his affairs, but he was helpless even when publishers followed him to such remote places as Saranac Lake, New York. In 1887 S. S. McClure went there to offer him $8,000 for a serial and to convey Joseph Pulitzer's offer of $10,000 a year for a brief weekly article. Stevenson presently had to write to Charles Scribner in New York City:

Heaven help me, I am under a curse just now. I have played fast and loose with what I said to you; and that, I beg you to believe, in the purest innocence of mind. I told you you should have the power over all my work in this country; and about a fortnight ago, when McClure was here, I calmly signed a bargain for the serial publication of a story. You will scarcely believe that I did this in mere oblivion; but I did; and all that I can say is that I will do so no more, and ask you to forgive me.

Scribner replied that what distressed him most was Stevenson's distress. And the following year, McClure named his new child Robert Louis McClure. Neither seems to have suggested that Stevenson needed a professional agent.

The first extended statement on behalf of literary agency was apparently the interview with A. P. Watt in 1892. Three years later friend Nicoll wrote an account of agency for the *Bookman* (New York). Nicoll recommends agency as a good business to be in: a small office will do, no capital is needed, selling a popular author is easy, and the 10 per cent fee provides a continuing income. (He must have written this solely for William Heinemann's benefit.) He thinks the agent is here to stay in spite of recalcitrant publishers, and he credits the agent with getting a general rise in authors' royalties from 10 per cent to 15 per cent and more. A popular author, whose books are expected to sell above twenty thousand copies, can now obtain 25 per cent royalty. Nicoll recalls a popular novel that was sold outright to the publisher for £500. Today, seventeen years later, the ledger of the publisher shows a profit of £19,000. The agent is making such robbery more difficult. In an article on 'Authors and Publishers' a few months later, Nicoll reports that Hall Caine is getting a royalty of 33⅓ per cent on his new novel. The book will have to sell thirty thousand copies before the publisher makes a penny. This is the contract that brought Gosse's comment about 'unbridled greed'. Nicoll laments the stealing of authors that is going on among almost all the publishers—a new phenomenon, he says, and one that occasionally results in ruinous royalties. But he does not put any blame upon the agents.

Two years later, George Haven Putnam devoted thirty pages of *Authors and Publishers* to the agents. He made the usual points against agency, but thought that with serial publication the agent was well nigh indispensable. His experience suggested that agents were most active in England, less so in France, still less in America and Germany. In 1899 in *The Pen and the Book* Walter Besant also decided that the agents were indispensable, and he was now of the opinion that they came into being because the Society of Authors published *The Cost of Publishing*. At about this time the writers of authors' manuals began to contemplate the agent, and one of the first to do so expressed qualified approval: E. H. Lacon Watson in *Hints to Young Authors* in 1902. In Watson's view, the agents can rarely help the beginner, they have too commercial an eye, and they are sometimes reported to serve editors and publishers instead of authors; but they can sell what the author cannot in the respect that they know the market—which magazines are full up and which are not, and which publisher wants what—and in Watson's own experience they have gone to great pains to help him. Use the agent, says Watson, but do not become his hack: it may pay, but it will be boring. A year later E. A. Bennett had much the same thing to say.

7

As a writer and editor with ten years of experience behind him, and with a fairly wide acquaintance among editors and publishers, he spoke with a good deal of authority; and for him the agent question was a settled question: 'The editor and the publisher who "cannot understand why authors should be so foolish as to pay 10 per cent of their earnings to an agent" are marked men in genuine literary circles.' He thought that on the average a rising young author who put his work into the hands of an agent would double his income within a year. The author should not rely heavily on his agent's literary advice, but once minimum prices were settled between them, he should rely entirely on him in business opinion.

The year 1905 brought an encomium to agents by the publisher F. V. White in an interview in *Publisher and Bookseller*: 'I am glad ... [of] an opportunity of testifying to the unbroken satisfaction and cordiality which has marked my dealings with agents ... [for] the last twenty years.' On another page the editors express their approval of White's remarks, and think that most of the unkind things that are said of the agents are untrue. A year later, Curtis Brown replied to Henry Holt's strictures on agents in an unsigned article in the *Fortnightly Review*. The bogus agent, said Brown, presents no problem to anyone but the author: the publishers know who he is, and return his manuscripts unread. The real agent has a real task: to see that a sound and honest bargain is made, one that is profitable to both author and publisher and of special advantage to neither. The agent who can perform such a task will flourish.

Naturally enough, the pleasantest defence of literary agency came from the pen of Arnold Bennett, whose excellent relations with J. B. Pinker eventually enabled him to maintain a yacht with a crew of eight. The basis of the defence can be seen in the correspondence between the two men (*Letters of Arnold Bennett*, Volume I), whose high point is a letter from Bennett of 20 June 1906. He had written earlier to Pinker to tell him he was engaged to be married, and Pinker responded warmly. Bennett then wrote: 'I can't let this occasion pass without expressing to you my deep sense of your excellence as an agent & your good value as a friend. I do not often give vent to my feelings, but I am in a highly emotional state just now, & I use the chance to tell you what I think. Pinker, I will write

you some *books* in the future!' Bennett's engagement collapsed but
his promise to Pinker did not, and *The Old Wives' Tale* was begun
sixteen months later. In the following year, in one of his 'Books
and Persons' essays in the *New Age*, Bennett made a public defence
of agency. He has heard, he says, that the book season has been bad
and that one publisher has had to reduce his staff of twenty gardeners
to eighteen. (This would be A. M. S. Methuen, who was soon to
become Bennett's own publisher.) Every time Bennett goes into a
publisher's office a literary agent has just left, 'gorged with illicit
gold'. Bennett would like to meet that agent. He has never known
an agent to get the better of a publisher, and is prepared to offer
£50 for the name of one: 'Such a literary agent is badly wanted.'
Publishers have always made more money out of books than authors,
and always will, and the lucky thing today is that authors are paid
better than they were twenty years ago. If the book season is bad,
Bennett would like to see those people suffer who can most afford to.

In making such comments on publishers, Bennett doubtless took
pleasure in his pseudonym for his 'Books and Persons' column:
Jacob Tonson. He capped his opinions a few years later in a letter to
the *Author* in July 1913. The previous month the *Author* had published a letter by H. G. Wells attacking the agents. Wells had been
one of J. B. Pinker's first clients but quarrelled with him and quarrelled later with other agents. In his letter he spoke of being plagued
by agents who wanted to handle his business. He concluded: 'I know
of no way of stopping this increasing nuisance of agents, except by
proclaiming clearly that, like all sensible authors, I do not employ
agents except for specific jobs.' Bennett's letter read:

> So long as my friend Wells is content to speak for himself about agents
> I am ready to listen in respectful silence, but when he begins to speak
> for 'all sensible authors', I must protest. I maintain that I am a sensible
> author. If lampoonists and satirists are to be believed, I have a reputation
> for considerable business acumen. Bluntly, I think this reputation is
> deserved.
> As one 'sensible author', I wish to 'proclaim clearly' that I should not
> dream of employing agents only 'for specific jobs'. On the contrary I am
> absolutely convinced that every author of large and varied output ought
> to put the whole of his affairs into the hands of a good agent, and that
> every such author who fails to do so loses money by his omission. I admit

that some agents are bad. I know that some are good. A good agent will do a specific job better than an author, partly because he knows the market better, and partly because he is an expert in the diplomacy of bargains. But a good agent is also very valuable in utilising opportunities as they arise—opportunities of whose very existence the author is ignorant. I reckon that in the latter activity alone a good agent recoups an author again and again for the whole of his commission.

In my experience it is precisely when agents are employed only for 'specific jobs' that trouble comes.

Wells, my senior, once advised—nay, commanded—me to go to an agent. With my usual docility I did so. I have never regretted it. I have never had the slightest agency trouble as the result of following Wells' advice. I am quite sure that if I had not followed his advice I should be very decidedly worse off than I am. My gratitude to Wells is lasting. That happened some thirteen years ago. Experience has led Wells to change his views. Experience has only confirmed me in my views, formerly his. He may be right; I may be wrong. I will not dogmatise. But he must not speak for 'all sensible authors'.

Wells replied the following month: 'I deplore my forgotten advice . . . How are we to prove these things . . . ? I must talk privately to E.A.B. in this connexion.' Several years later, Wells was given the *coup de grâce*. In the endpapers of *The Authors' Handbook for 1935* there appeared several advertisements by literary agents, among them A. P. Watt; and Watt's advertisement consisted solely of a letter to the senior member of the firm from a satisfied author. The letter was dated 5 October 1926, and had duly appeared in earlier issues of the firm's *Collection of Letters*. It read:

My dear Watt,

I have not always done my business through an agent; most literary agents I regard with suspicion faintly tinged with derision; but there can be no doubt that such agency as *your* firm can give—I refuse altogether any general benediction upon agents—becomes of great and increasing value as a writer's distinction becomes apparent. . . . We have been allies in recent years in regard to my work, and I very gladly bear my testimony to the fact that your commercial value to me has been out of all proportion greater than the commission you have charged me. . . .

Very sincerely yours,
H. G. Wells.

During these years a few more agents spoke in their own behalf. In 1911 the Literary Agency of London (later absorbed by Curtis

Brown) replied in the *Author* to George Bernard Shaw's argument that it paid the agent to make a dozen contracts with a 10 or 15 per cent royalty instead of one or two at 20 per cent. True enough, they said, but agents have to take an even longer view than Shaw credits them with taking: they have to look to their reputations, and agents who make contracts unsatisfactory to their authors will lose their authors. In 1925 appeared an authoritative if brief account of agency by Michael Joseph, who made an unusual progress from journalist to agent to publisher. He was Director of the Curtis Brown agency from 1926 to 1935. His account is part of one of his writers' guides, *The Commercial Side of Literature*. He agrees that the agent cannot help the beginner, for no agent has the time that the beginner has. Otherwise the agent is invaluable because he knows the market and the problems and rights of contracts as no writer is likely to know them. And the agent is as valuable to the publisher as to the author, and most publishers know it. The agent sifts the chaff from the wheat, rejecting—in the instance known to Joseph—85 per cent of the manuscripts submitted by authors; and the publishers who receive the remainder have the benefit of a valued opinion. By the same token, a publisher discounts the recommendation of an agent whom he does not respect. The market for good literature far exceeds the supply, and publishers regularly make known their wants to the half dozen agents of substantial reputation.

In the thirties the attacks on agents in the *Author* drew responses from several agents. Curtis Brown thought that the more successful the author, the more difficult the task of the agent, for there then arose all the complications of cinema, radio, second serial, translation, and even toy rights. And the more successful the author, the more valuable his time and hence the greater need for the services of an agent. Raymond Savage (a onetime associate of Curtis Brown and then of Hughes Massie) ridiculed the notion that a professional fee would be better than a 10 per cent charge. The young writer could not afford such fees, and the 10 per cent charge enabled the agent to work for him for nothing and receive payment later. Savage offered to draw up a scale of fees for services and during the next year to deal with every new author according to them. Would the Society of Authors guarantee his losses if the authors could not afford to pay?

Audrey Heath (of A. M. Heath) wondered why the young author who gratefully paid his agent £5 on a desperately needed £50 sale was later reluctant to pay £100 on an unneeded £1,000 sale. The author forgot that on the £50 sale the agent lost money: £5 would not pay for reading a manuscript, writing letters about it, delivering it to publishers, and consulting author and publisher about it when it was taken.

The attacks and responses in the *Author* ended with a letter from a writer and ex-publisher, Alec Waugh. Waugh wrote in to say that when he was on the Board of Directors of Chapman and Hall he had cordial relations with all the main agents and became the friend of a few. He was always aware, though, that they kept the interests of their authors uppermost. 'Chapman and Hall enjoys a high reputation for cooperative generosity towards its authors, but I have no hesitation in saying that those authors who dealt with us through agents got better terms than those who dealt directly.' He instanced the agents' rejection of the 13 as 12 clause around the end of the First World War. The clause, a standard one in contracts prior to that time, stipulated that every thirteen books delivered by the publisher to the bookseller would count as twelve in the paying of royalties. The removal of this clause alone virtually paid the commission that the author surrendered to his agent. Likewise when publishers dealt with authors directly, they usually invited them to hand over 25 per cent of American and film rights. The agents reduced this figure to 10 per cent. Waugh thought that more than 97 per cent of the work of the big agents was conducted on behalf of authors, less than 3 per cent conducted explicitly on behalf of publishers. His general viewpoint echoed that of his father a few years before in *A Hundred Years of Publishing*, in which high praise was given to the integrity and capability of A. P. Watt, J. B. Pinker, and C. F. Cazenove (of the Literary Agency of London). Particularly Pinker,

. . . whose shrewdness and knowledge of what the public wants were invaluable to his authors, while his lively sense of humour, and flow of anecdote, were apt to render his visit to a publisher so beguiling that, before he knew where he was, the man of business would find that he had suddenly agreed to terms which ten minutes before he had no intention of conceding.

The years must have mellowed Arthur Waugh's recollection of his quarrel with Pinker and Arnold Bennett (recorded in some detail in *Letters of Arnold Bennett*, Volume I), but that quarrel itself showed author and agent on one side and publisher on the other. Still, the last word on whether agents served publishers more than they served authors should hardly have been left to a publisher and an ex-publisher. In any event the public quarrelling died out with the thirties.

VIII No Ending: Literary Agency and the Complaining Author Today

> The chief glory of every people arises from its authors.
> —Samuel Johnson, *Dictionary*, 1755

At a dinner of the Society of Authors in 1905, Sir Arthur Conan Doyle noted that a well-known writer on astronomy left an estate of £1,200, a well-known writer on zoology left £300, and a well-known publisher left £750,000. Unfair! cried the editors of *Publisher and Bookseller*. Everyone knows that Mr. George Smith of Smith, Elder made his fortune not from books but from Apollinaris mineral water. His generosity to authors was proverbial, and he spent a huge sum on the *Dictionary of National Biography* without getting half of it back. (But was it true that he gave Dante Gabriel Rossetti only £9 for *Early Italian Poets*? and how much in fact did he make from books?) In 1926 Sir Stanley Unwin reflected upon the estates left by several categories of persons. He did not particularly want to generalize, but he could not resist putting the figures into *The Truth About Publishing*. Arnold Bennett and Sir Arthur Conan Doyle have here been added to his list.

Publishers	John Lane	£12,000
	William Heinemann	£33,000
	J. M. Dent	£14,000
Booksellers	J. J. Banks	£35,000
	B. H. Blackwell	£54,000
Authors	Charles Garvice	£71,000
	Rider Haggard	£61,000
	Sir Henry Lucy	£250,000
	Arnold Bennett	£36,000
	Conan Doyle	£63,000
Agents	J. B. Pinker	£40,000
	A. P. Watt	£60,000
Weekly Newspaper Proprietor	Sir William Ingram	£265,000

Pity the poor publisher!

The truth about literary agency is equally hard to come by. In 1930 Arthur Waugh remarked that most publishers had long since accepted the agents. Heinemann, said Waugh, was the exception, a publisher who early in his career was mortally offended by an agent's taking away a valued writer, and he swore never to deal with agents again. Are we then to infer that Heinemann's attack on agents and on A. P. Watt in particular in 1893 tells us more about Heinemann himself than about the problems of literary agency? At the end of his attack, Heinemann makes an exception of the Authors' Syndicate, which was headed by his friend, W. M. Colles. There is some reason to believe that the author stolen from Heinemann was Rudyard Kipling, who published one of his books with Heinemann in 1892 and was married to the wife of an associate of Heinemann's who died that year. Kipling is described in Charles Morgan's *The House of Macmillan* as a man with a fundamental distrust of publishers. Was Kipling's praise for his agent—Watt—in his letter to the *Athenaeum* merely a fine example of such distrust? Perhaps Heinemann's animus was fair, and was doubly fair in 1918 when W. P. Watt tried to take away some of his young authors. When he died in 1920 he left half of his estate for the encouragement of poetry and other unprofitable kinds of writing.

Even when personalities were kept out of it, the argument over agency reached no easy conclusion. One disputant asserted that the interests of author and agent were identical because the higher the royalty the agent got for his author, the higher the pay he himself received. True enough, said Shaw, but in the long run the agent will make more money for himself if he settles a dozen contracts quickly at 10 per cent instead of arguing out two at 20. Yes, said the Literary Agency of London, but such an agent will eventually lose his authors. Quite so, someone else said, except that for centuries publishers underpaid their authors without losing them, and agents do the same.

The argument was of course academic, whether it was personal or abstract. That level-headed and experienced editor and author, Arnold Bennett himself, said in 1903 that the agent question was no longer a vexed question but a settled question, and he was right. The causes for the rise of the agent had done their work, and no forceful examples or cleverly taken points would alter the fact one jot. A. P. Watt had his difficulties, but the success of his enterprise seems never to have been in doubt, and dozens of writers came to him in his first ten or fifteen years. Likewise the paths of his later rivals, J. B. Pinker and Curtis Brown, seem to have been altogether easy. After the fluctuations between totals of two and six agents in London from 1874 to 1894 (as given in the *Post Office Directory*), there comes a steady rise to the more than seventy agents today. Such a rough index must be complemented by the fact that an estimated 90 per cent of agency work today is carried out by the five leading agencies. Watt himself dominated the field in such a way for the first twenty years; and then, without losing in volume of work, began to share the domination with Pinker in 1896 and Brown at the turn of the century. Curtis Brown today, probably the largest agency in London, employs more than fifty people; in 1910 it employed perhaps half a dozen. Pinker employed such a number at that time, and his son doubled the figure in the twenties. Sir Stanley Unwin estimated in 1926 that less than 50 per cent of the annual publication of twelve thousand books passed through the hands of agents. A recent writer put the current figure at 75 per cent. The argument over agency preoccupied the attention of a few people; the great majority said nothing, at least in print; and the agents flourished.

Presumably the argument had some bearing on the character of agency, though it is difficult to see a direct influence. The Society of Authors repeatedly urged the formation of an association of agents so that a general code of conduct could be enforced. In the late twenties one of the agents, Raymond Savage, made the attempt and failed. He reported that the three biggest agencies refused to support such an organization, others were suspicious of it, and too many of the remainder were the incompetent and unscrupulous agents who had everything to lose by joining. In 1937 he tried again, and met with the same refusal by the big three; but he joined with two other firms to form the Society of Literary Agents, and hoped for success. The Society failed, and no other organization has taken its place. Why the three major agencies should have remained aloof is not entirely clear; but one of them, the Curtis Brown firm, was wrenched in two in the thirties when Nancy Pearn, Laurence Pollinger, and David Higham left to found their own firm, and the second of the big three, the Pinker firm, crashed at the end of the decade. Doubtless jealousy and self-protection militated against union. All the same, the major agencies have perhaps always offered contracts to their authors that were similar to and sometimes more liberal than the contract proposed by the Society of Authors in 1912 (see page 84). The Curtis Brown agency today has no formal contracts with its authors, who are free to take back their 10 per cent tomorrow. The agency says that it relies upon satisfactory service to see that they do not. The agency submits contracts for approval, collects royalties, and deducts the 10 per cent fee, which is a comprehensive fee. Variations from this standard depend upon the wishes and bargaining power of the individual author.

The material success of literary agency has to some extent changed its function, or changed the way its function is seen. When Alec Waugh said in 1937 that less than 3 per cent of the work of the major agents was for publishers, he was referring to explicit employment, and his figure would not have allayed fear of gentlemen's agreements between agents and publishers against their authors. Nevertheless the fear went underground, and the agent today has no hesitation in describing his activity as of utmost service to both authors and publishers. (Like most of his predecessors he is something more than a 'true agent'.) Paul Reynolds, Jr., estimated in the fifties that the *Saturday Evening Post* took 80 per cent of its material through agents; and Spencer Curtis Brown more recently estimated that aside from the work of established writers, publishers took the same percentage of manuscripts his firm submitted. This latter 80 per cent represented eight of ten manuscripts from a total of a thousand received by the agency. In the view of a writer in the *Economist*, the agents 'act as a sieve through which a large proportion of the flood of incoming manuscripts is shortlisted'. The publisher is relieved of work, and has the benefit of an agent's opinion on what is forwarded.[1] Since the publisher must deal with the agent for the

1 The article ('The Author's Friend', *Economist*, 25 July 1959) says that of the thousand manuscripts, the agent tries to place one hundred, and succeeds with three or four. Geoffrey Faber, in *A Publisher Speaking*, London, 1934, reports similar figures from an agent. In Mr. Brown's opinion, such an agent would go bankrupt. [*cont.*]

work of most established writers, reliance on the agent is considerable. Likewise, of the goodly number of ideas for books that germinate in the minds of publishers, very many are conveyed to willing authors by the agents. Most important, perhaps, is the fact that the increasing internationalization of literature since the Second World War and the proliferation of sources and outlets for copyright have meant that book publication is sometimes only the beginning of profits; and the agent's exploration of radio, cinema, television, gramophone, and other rights can be vastly profitable to the publisher as well as to the author and the agent himself. In a complex and commercial world, the agent seems to have a secure and necessary place.

If the question of literary agency has been answered by history, another question remains unsolved—the one that some people thought literary agency itself would solve: the plight of the author. Literary agency has helped to raise the average royalty rate of authors, has opened new markets to individual authors, is a virtual necessity to full-time authors; yet authors remain poor. There is vastly more money to be made in books today than a hundred years ago, and there are agents to explore markets undreamed of then; but the publisher takes 50 to 60 per cent on the price of a book, the bookseller takes a third, and the author takes 10 or 15 per cent, giving one tenth of that to the agent. Moreover, the publisher and bookseller take their sums from hundreds of books, and the author takes his from the five, ten, twenty, forty, or eighty that he can write. The agent, drawing his tenth of a tenth, but drawing it from a good many writers, likewise does better than the author. The two most significant figures in Sir Stanley Unwin's enlarged list are those for J. B. Pinker and Arnold Bennett. Here is the cleverest agent of his time, with a client who is one of the most prolific and

---

To what extent the publisher is genuinely relieved of work by the agent is unclear, since unpublished writers are perhaps likely to try publishers directly before they go to agents, and many unpublished writers apparently do not try agents at all. In an article in the *Guardian* in 1966 David McKie says that publishers estimate that six or seven manuscripts in every thousand are accepted, and agents estimate ten in every thousand. He supposes that the discrepancy reflects the fact that publishers receive all the unpublished manuscripts that do and do not reach the agents.

businesslike of major writers: the agent's estate after about twenty-five years of business is £40,000, and the client's after more than thirty-five of writing is £36,000. The still more significant figures are missing from the list: the estates of ordinary writers on Grub Street. If Gissing tried to paint too dark a picture of the 1880s, there was nevertheless no room for complacency then, and there is none today.

In 1966 Richard Findlater drew together the results of an investigation into the financial condition of authors conducted by the Society of Authors. His pamphlet, *The Book Writers: Who Are They?*, begins with the acknowledgement that much of Britain's great literature was written under hardship and may even have been inspired by hardship. Who is to say that great writers of the future would not be killed by kindness? Findlater's figures indicate that there may be no need to worry on the latter score.[1] Fifty per cent of the members of the Society of Authors responded to the inquiry, 1,587 out of 3,240. Of this number 46 per cent reported themselves as full-time authors and another 10 per cent reported themselves as nearly full-time. The average income of these two groups for the years 1963–5 was well below £500 per annum, less than the minimum pay of a bus driver. Only about half of them did earn as much as £500. From book rights and subsidiary rights in drama, television, translation, etc., about one-sixth of all the 1,587 authors earned more than £1,050 a year, and two-thirds earned less than £312. Most of the authors involved, says Findlater, 'are not novices and hacks, but educated and experienced writers, each with a number of books to his or her credit.'

Findlater then takes a look into the future, and he finds the commercial scene unpromising. Too much of Britain's expanding book

1 The situation is different in America, where literature is taken seriously and where money abounds. Journals of higher criticism there occasionally remark upon the fortunate fact that more and more trained observers in the academy are on the lookout for literary talent. Almost every university in America is pleased to offer creative writing courses and to keep a creative writer or two in harness. Numerous private and governmental organizations (from the Guggenheim Foundation to the Central Intelligence Agency) provide funds for authors and publishers alike. And much of this virtue is stultifying when it is not sinister. The contrast between English indifference and American concern, and what each can do for the ordinary writer, is accurately and amusingly described in Malcolm Bradbury's novel *Stepping Westward*.

trade consists of overseas sales, where the author's reward drops precipitately; earnings from journalism, radio, television, and the cinema amount to no more than £60 to £70 a year for most book writers; the paperback market requires sales in the order of ten times the sales of hardcover books to provide equivalent royalties, and many books are either unsuitable for the paperback market or can earn only the most modest sums there. And what new schemes for improving the lot of authors do those modern patrons, the literary agents and the publishers, have in mind? Findlater says nothing of the agents, perhaps concurring with the long-held views on agency of the officials of the Society of Authors; but it is certain that the agents are not in the forefront of efforts to encourage new writers or to assist the profession as a whole. Of the publishers, Findlater says little that is encouraging. He notes that there are disreputable and occasionally respectable publishers who skimp on royalties, and that there are their opposites who take large risks with new writers and help maintain older writers. But what is needed is collective action, says Findlater, and the Publishers' Association seems unable to speak with the voice of many of its individually generous members. The Association has shown little concern to reduce publishing costs, to improve the bookselling system, to support assistance to authors out of funds from a governmental levy on books out of copyright.

The only genuine solution that Findlater sees is collective action by authors themselves, and he points to the Society of Authors as the ready instrument. Of course! Who could really expect publishers or literary agents or any other group to agitate to improve the lot of others at the possible expense of themselves? Yet as Findlater remarks at the outset of his discussion, authors tend to be 'loners, anti-joiners', having a 'deep-rooted . . . resistance to collective effort'. Despite recent notable efforts by the Society of Authors in behalf of library-usage royalties for authors, the Society is less powerful and less militant today than it was in the eighties and nineties, and its achievements then were modest.

Recently, under the generosity and cultural interest of enlightened Socialism, the annual awards of the Arts Council to authors rose from £15,000 to £65,000, and the cries of sorrow, derision, and outrage over this tribute to England's literary genius echoed through the pages of the *Times Literary Supplement*. Recently there gathered in Cheltenham an assortment of publishers, editors, agents, and authors to celebrate England's literary genius, and in the midst of the celebration an author who later acknowledged that he lived on baked beans rose and shouted, 'Codswallop'. Said Pendennis to Warrington: 'I protest against that wretch of a middleman whom I see between Genius and his great landlord, the Public.' The publisher flourishes, and so does the man who followed him into the middle. Authors protest, and the millennium is a long way off.

Bibliography on the Conditions of Authorship

Aside from the bibliographies in the *Cambridge Bibliography of English Literature*, there has been little effort made to draw together the literature on the conditions of authorship. The present list is very partial in certain respects: it does not include anything on copyright, publishers and publishing history, printers and printing history, patronage and the dedication of books, journalism, or the lives of authors, except such works as were used in writing this book. It covers general discussions of author–publisher relations, literature on the author's situation, and material on literary agency and the related activities of vanity publishing, newspaper agencies, and societies for authors. Occasional items are annotated. Several items listed were unseen, and they are so marked. The list includes everything that was used in preparing the book. + after a journal indicates only that the journal was published for at least several years.

The Academy (London). 1, 8, 15 January 1898, letters by Walter Besant, William Heinemann, and Alfred Nutt regarding publishing expenses.

Additional Letters on the Bookselling Question, 1852, London, [1852]. Pamphlet. See below, *The Opinions of Certain Authors*.

'The Agent Question', *Bulletin of the Authors' League of America*, II (April 1914), 6–9.

'Agents' Fees', *Bulletin of the Authors' League of America*, II (January 1915), 9–10.

Albright, Evelyn May. 'Notes on the Status of Literary Property, 1500–1545', *Modern Philology*, XVII (December 1919), 439–55.

Aldis, H. G. 'Book Production and Distribution, 1625–1800', *Cambridge History of English Literature*, XI, Cambridge, 1914, 311–42.

——. 'The Book Trade, 1557–1625', *Cambridge History of English Literature*, IV, Cambridge, 1910, 378–414.

Allen, Clarence E. *Publishers' Accounts*, London, 1897. To remedy commonly inadequate accounting; chapter on literary property.

Allen, Frederick Lewis. *Paul Revere Reynolds*, New York, 1944.

Altick, Richard. *The Art of Literary Research*, New York, 1963. Pp. 27–34 on authors' prices.

——. *The English Common Reader*, Chicago, 1963. Nineteenth-century reading public.

'Amateur Authors and Bogus Publishers', *Tit-Bits*, XVIII (28 June 1890), 187.

Andrews, William. *Literary Byways*, London, 1898. Chapter on authors' earnings.

Anecdotes of Books and Authors, London, 1836. Chapter on poverty of authors.

Arber, Edward. *A Transcript of the Registers of the Company of Stationers of London*, London, 1875-7.

Arnold, Matthew. 'Copyright', in *Irish Essays*, London, 1882.

Association to Protect the Rights of Authors. Issued a report, unseen. Information on Association in *Publishers' Circular*, 2 April 1875; *Athenaeum*, 13 March 1875, pp. 359-61, and 15 May 1875, p. 655; *The Times*, 25 March 1875 and later. See also below, Moy Thomas.

[?Atall, John] *The Adventures of an Author, Written by Himself and a Friend*, London, 1767. Picaresque; only occasional references to authorship.

The Athenaeum (London). Almost week by week a valuable source of information on the conditions of authors. Some especially important material appears on the following dates: 3, 10, 17 February 1883 (on author-publisher); 3 December 1892-25 February 1893 (on hardships of publishing; see William Heinemann below); 14 October -11 November 1893 (Besant *v.* publishers); 11-18 November 1893 (Heinemann on agents); 16 February-16 March 1895 (a quarrel between an author, a publisher, and the Society of Authors).

Atto, Clayton. 'The Society for the Encouragement of Learning', *The Library*, 4th Ser., XIX (December 1938), 263-88.

The Author, London, 1854. Poem in 4 books on the pains and glories of authorship.

The Author (Boston, 1889-92, and then merged with *The Writer*). Only vol. II seen; brief but useful articles on authors' finances in March, June, July, August, September, December.

The Author (London, 1890+). Month by month the most valuable source of information on agents; much on the author's situation generally. Some important items appear on the following dates: 15 May 1890 (Edmund Gosse's essay from *The Grievances Between Authors*, which see); 15 November 1890 (Gosse on writing as a trade); 2 May 1892 (on agents); 1 September 1893 (Walter Besant on author-publisher); 1 October 1901 (William Heinemann on agents); 1 April 1904 (G. H. Thring on agents); 1 July 1905 (G. B. Shaw on publishers); 1 November 1906 (on agents); 1 July 1909 (on agents); 1 March 1911 (on agents); 1 October 1911 (on agents); 1 November 1911 (on Society for the Encouragement of Learning); 1 December 1911 (May Sinclair, G. B. Shaw, and others on agents); 1 March 1912 (on agents); 1 June-1 October 1913 (H. G. Wells, Arnold Bennett, Hall Caine on agents); January 1926 (on Curtis Brown); April 1926 (Curtis Brown replies); Summer 1932 (Hugh Walpole, Marie Belloc Lowndes, and others on agents); Autumn 1932 (Curtis Brown, Raymond Savage, and others replying); Winter 1932 (Laurence Housman and others on agents); Summer 1937 (on agents); Autumn 1937 (on Curtis Brown; Alec Waugh on agents); Christmas 1939 (on agents).

The Authoress. A Tale, London, 1819. Parody, with explanations, of circulating library fiction.

The Authors' and Booksellers' Cooperative Equitable Publishing Alliance, Limited, London, 1901. The author offers shares in a company in which authors and booksellers might combine to beat the publishers.

The Author's Annual, 1929, New York, 1929. Also issued 1930; chapter on the business side of writing.

The Authors' Circular (London, 1898). The official organ of the English School of Journalism. Proposes to be an efficient medium in which authors and literary agents can advertise their wares to publishers—through paid advertisements.

The Author's Complaint, Edinburgh, [1832 ?]. Satiric sheet against people who ridicule the publishing of verses.

'The Author's Friend', *Economist*, CXCII (25 July 1959), 202–3. On agents.

The Author's Guide, London, [*c.* 1900]. Issued by West, Newman & Co. Unseen.

The Author's Guide to Printing and Publishing, [1886]. 2nd ed. Unseen.

The Author's Hand-Book, London, 1844. (3rd ed. 1845.) From a vanity publisher, E. Churton.

The Authors' Handbook, 1939, London, 1939. First issued 1934; contains article on agency, pp. 339–43.

Authorship and Publication: A Concise Guide for Authors, London, 1882. From Wyman & Sons.

The Authors' League of America, Privately printed, 1912. Pamphlet.

The Authors' Note Book and Literary Gossip (London, 1876–7). Journal proposing to be wailing wall for authors.

The Authors of the Town; A Satire Inscribed to the Author of the Universal Passion, London, 1725. Poem attacking gentlemen authors and hack writers.

The Author's Review, and Literary Protector (London, 1812). See below, *Prospectus*.

The Author's Triumph: or The Manager Managed, London, 1737. A farce that touches upon the poverty of authors.

Baines, Jocelyn. *Joseph Conrad*, London, 1960. Material on J. B. Pinker.

The Ballantyne Press and Its Founders, 1796–1908, Edinburgh, 1909.

Barnes, James. *Free Trade in Books*, Oxford, 1964. Book-pricing in nineteenth century; Chapter 5 concerns authors involved in issue.

Barrie, J. M. *The Author*, Cincinnati, n.d. (Reprinted from the *Scots Observer*, 28 June 1890.)

Barrie, J. M. *Letters*, ed. Viola Meynell, London, 1942. Letters to Golding Bright.

Bartlett, Paul Alexander. 'Letters of Ford Madox Ford', *Saturday Review of Literature*, XXIV (2 August 1941), 3–4, 14. Some letters to J. B. Pinker.

Baxter, Richard. *Reliquiae Baxterianae*, London, 1696. Appendix VII, 117–18, on B.'s relations with publisher.

Bennett, Arnold. *Books and Persons*, London, 1917. Several pieces on authors, agents, and publishers.

——. *How to Become an Author*, London, 1903.

——. *Journals*, 3 vols., London, 1932–3. References to J. B. Pinker.

——. *Letters*, I (Letters to J. B. Pinker), ed. James Hepburn, London and New York, 1966.

Bennett, H. S. *English Books & Readers, 1476 to 1557*, Cambridge, 1952.

——. *English Books & Readers, 1558 to 1603*, Cambridge, 1965.

Besant, Sir Walter. *Autobiography*, London, 1902. Material on A. P. Watt.

——. 'Literature as a Career', *Forum*, XIII (August 1892), 693–708.

——. 'On Some Difficulties of the Young Author', *Illustrated London News*, XCVIII (7 February 1891), 186.

——. *The Pen and the Book*, London, 1899. Chapter on agency.

——. *The Society of Authors. A Record of its Actions from its Foundation*, London, 1893.

——. 'The Work of the British Society of Authors', *Forum*, XIII (March 1892), 95–106.

——. See also under *The Academy*, *The Athenaeum*, *The Author* (London), and *The Grievances Between Authors*.

Birrell, Augustine. *The Law and History of Copyright in Books*, London, 1899.

Blagden, Cyprian. *The Stationers' Company*, Cambridge, Mass., 1960.

Blanchard, Laman. *Sketches from Life*, 3 vols., New York, 1846. Includes memoir by Bulwer Lytton on the difficulties of the lives of authors, Blanchard's in particular.

Bond, Richmond P. 'John Partridge and the Company of Stationers', *Studies in Bibliography*, XVI (1963), 61–80. Almanac-maker *v.* publishers.

Books and Authors, Edinburgh, [1868]. Some material on pains and poverty of authors.

The Bookseller, 1816. Poem; unseen.

The Book World, London, 1935. Chapter on agency.

The Book World Today, ed. John Hampden, London, 1957. Chapter on author–agent–publisher.

Booth, William Stoke. *A Practical Guide for Authors*, Boston and New York, 1907.

Brabrook, Edward W. *The Royal Society of Literature of the United Kingdom. A Brief Account of its Origin and Progress*, London, 1897.

Bradbury, Malcolm. *Stepping Westward*, London, 1965. Novel about English author in America.

'The Brain-Sucker: Or, The Distress of Authorship. A Serio-Comic Caricature', *British Mercury*, No. 1 (12 May 1787), pp. 14–27; No. 2 (May 1787), pp. 43–8. (Reprinted in a new edition of the first four numbers issued as single volume, London, 1788.) A farmer recounts how his son went mad and then went to London and became a hack writer.

Brittain, Vera. *On Being an Author*, New York, 1948.

Brooks, C. H. and Heath, Audrey. 'The Agent's Point of View', *Authors' Handbook, 1939*, London, 1939, pp. 429–32. Not in 1935 edition.

[Brown, Curtis] ' "The Commercialisation of Literature" and the Literary Agent', *Fortnightly Review*, LXXX (1 August 1906), 355–63.

Brown, Curtis. *Contacts*, London, 1935. Memoirs.

——. See *The Author* (London).

Brown, ——. *A Plea for the Book Agent*, 1903. Unseen.

Brydges, Sir Egerton. *Answer to the Further Statement, Ordered by the Syndics of the University of Cambridge*, London, 1818. Response to the Syndics on copyright issue.

——. *Reasons for a Farther Amendment of the Act 54 Geo. III. c. 156, Being an Act to Amend the Copyright Act of Queen Anne*, London, 1817. (Also in *Pamphleteer*, x (1817), 493–507.)

——. *A Summary Statement of the Great Grievances Imposed on Authors and Publishers: and the Injury Done to Literature, by the Late Copyright Act*, London, 1818.

Buchanan, Robert. 'Is Barabbas a Necessity?' See below, Harriett Jay.

Buckler, William. *Matthew Arnold's Books: Toward a Publishing Diary*, Geneva, 1958. A.'s correspondence with Macmillan and Smith, Elder.

The Bulletin of the Authors' League of America (New York, 1913+). A few important items listed separately.

Burt, Robert C. 'A Dealer in Brains, Major J. B. Pond and His Associates', *Pearson's Magazine*, v (January 1898), 75–82.

Burtis, Mary Elizabeth. *Moncure Conway*, New Brunswick, 1952.

Bush, Douglas. 'Seventeenth Century Authorship', *Mint*, 11 (1948), 138–51.

Caine, Hall. See *The Author* (London).

Carlyle, Thomas. See *The Opinions of Certain Authors*.

[Carte, Thomas] *Farther Reasons Humbly Offered to the Consideration of the Honourable House of Commons, for Making More Effectual an Act . . . for the Encouragement of Learning, by Vesting the Copies of Printed Books in the Authors or Purchasers of Such Copies during the Times Therein Mentioned*, [c. 1737]. Recommends extending author's copyright beyond 14 years, also controlling importation of English books produced abroad. Title of pamphlet given somewhat differently in Nichols, *Literary Anecdotes*, II, 508, possibly another edition.

——. *Proposals for Publishing by Subscription, an History of the Life of James Duke of Ormonde*, London, 1733.

The Case of Authors and Proprietors of Books, [1753?]. Pamphlet; argues the author's right to his work.

The Case of the Booksellers and Printers Stated; with Answers to the Objections of the Patentee, 1666. A single sheet attacking the monopoly held by John Moore in printing books dealing with the Common Law.

Catalogue of a Collection of Works on Publishing and Bookselling in the British Library of Political and Economic Science, London, 1936. Includes unpublished items such as letter-books of the Authors' Syndicate.

A Century of Writers, 1855–1955, intro. Oliver Warner, London, 1955. Author–publisher material in introduction.

Chapman, John. *The Bookselling System*, [1852]. Pamphlet. Chapman himself was involved in the underselling of books. See below, *The Opinions of Certain Authors*.

Chapman, R. W. 'Authors and Booksellers', in *Johnson's England*, ed. A. S. Turberville, II, Oxford, 1933, 310–30.

Charvat, William. *Literary Publishing in America, 1790–1850*, Philadelphia, 1959. Chapter on authors and publishers.

'A Chat with Mr. Eveleigh Nash', *Publisher and Bookseller*, 13 January 1906, pp. 322–3.

'A Chat with Mr. F. V. White', *Publisher and Bookseller*, 29 July 1905, pp. 410–11. Publisher on agency.

'Chat with Mr. William Swan Sonnenschein', *Publisher and Bookseller*, 6 May 1905, 146–7. Publisher on agency.

Charteris, Hon. Evan. *The Life and Letters of Sir Edmund Gosse*, London, 1931.

Church, Alfred J. 'Authors and Publishers', *Nineteenth Century*, LXI (May 1907), 852–9.

Churchill, Charles. *The Author, a Poem*, London, 1764.

Collection of Letters Addressed to A. P. Watt by Various People, London, 1893. Later editions vary; those seen include 1894, 1896, 1898, 1924, 1929. 1893 reprints interview with F. W. (see below); 1896 reprints W. R. Nicoll on Watt (see below).

Collins, A. S. *Authorship in the Days of Johnson*, London, 1927.

——. *The Profession of Letters*, London, 1928.

Collins, James. 'The American Grub Street', *Atlantic Monthly*, XCIII (November 1906), 634–43.

Colvert, James B. 'Agent and Author: Ellen Glasgow's Letters to Paul Revere Reynolds', *Studies in Bibliography*, XIV (1961), 177–96.

Comprehensive Guide to Printing and Publishing, London, 1869. 10th ed. 1877; also 1897. From a vanity publisher, W. H. Collingridge,

City Press. Successor to *Pocket Printing Guide* (see below) of same firm.

'The Condition of the Author in England, Germany, and France', *Fraser's Magazine*, XXXV (March 1847), 285–95.

'Confessions of a Publisher's Reader', *Tit-Bits*, XVII (8 March 1890), 352.

Conrad, Jessie. *Joseph Conrad and His Circle*, New York, 1935. On J. B. Pinker, pp. 112, 228–30, 238–9, and elsewhere.

Conrad, Joseph. *Joseph Conrad, Letters to William Blackwood and David Meldrum*, ed. William Blackburn, Durham, North Carolina, 1958.

Constable, Thomas. *Archibald Constable and His Literary Correspondents*, 3 vols., Edinburgh, 1873.

Constitution of a Society, to Support Authors in Distress, [1790]. Royal Literary Fund.

Conway, Moncure D. *Autobiography*, 2 vols., New York, 1904.

Cook, E. T. 'Ruskin and His Books', *Strand Magazine*, XXIV (December 1902), 677–87. Author as publisher.

Coolidge, Theresa. 'D. H. Lawrence to His Agent', *More Books* (Bulletin of the Boston Public Library), 6th Ser., XXXIII (January 1948), 23–4. Negligible, quotes letters from collection edited by Aldous Huxley.

Cooper, Anthony Ashley. *Soliloquy: or, Advice to an Author*, London, 1710.

Copinger, Walter Arthur. *The Law of Copyright*, London, 1870. Thomas Hardy's 'literary agent' in his first dealings with publishers.

Copyright, National and International, from the Point of View of a Publisher, London, 1879.

The Cost of Publishing, London, 1891. 3rd ed. Issued by the Society of Authors.

The Court Authors Displayed, London, 1731. Only incidentally concerned with political hack writing. On that subject see the pages of the *Gentleman's Magazine* in 1731.

Cox, R. G. 'The Reviews and Magazines', *A Guide to English Literature*, VI, ed. Boris Ford, London, 1963, 188–204.

Crane, Stephen. *Stephen Crane: Letters*, ed. R. W. Stallman and Lilian Gilkes, New York, 1960. Letters to J. B. Pinker, also W. M. Colles ('Collis').

Curle, Richard. *The Last Twelve Years of Conrad*, London, 1928. Pp. 154–155, 158 on J. B. Pinker.

Dark, Sidney. *The Life of Sir Arthur Pearson*, London, n.d.

Darwin, Charles. See *The Opinions of Certain Authors*.

Davis, Elmer. *Some Aspects of the Economics of Authorship*, New York, 1940. Pamphlet.

Davis, Noel Pharr. *The Life of Wilkie Collins*, Urbana, Illinois, 1956. References to A. P. Watt.

Deacon's Composition and Style with a Complete Guide to All Matters

Connected with Printing and Publishing, ed. Robert D. Blackman, London, [1885]. 5th ed.

A Description of Publishing Methods and Arrangements, New York, 1855. 4th ed. Unseen.

Dickens, Charles. *The Letters of*, I, 1820–39, ed. Madeline House and Graham Storey, Oxford, 1965. Much on D.'s dealings with publishers.

[Didier, Eugene L.] *American Publishers and English Authors*, Baltimore, 1879. Pamphlet on piracy.

D'Israeli, Isaac. *Calamities of Authors*, 2 vols., London, 1812.

——. *Curiosities of Literature*, London, 1791. See especially 'Poverty of the Learned'.

——. *The Literary Character*, London, 1818. See especially Chapter 17.

——. *Quarrels of Authors*, 3 vols., London, 1814. See especially the Appendix to I.

Doran, George Henry. *Chronicles of Barabbas*, New York, 1935. Memoirs, pp. 94–5 on J. B. Pinker.

Drayton, Michael. *Poly-Olbion, The Second Part*, London, 1622. Prefatory note attacks stationers.

Dryden, John. *Letters*, ed. Charles E. Ward, Durham, North Carolina, 1942. Includes some correspondence with Jacob Tonson.

[Duppa, Richard] *An Address to the Parliament of Great Britain on the Claims of Authors to Their Own Copyright*, 1813. Unseen; apparently a 4th edition; the third, unpublished, edition is reprinted in *Pamphleteer*, II (1813), 169–202.

Eliot, George. *The George Eliot Letters*, 7 vols., ed. Gordon S. Haight, New Haven and London, 1954–5. Correspondence with publishers, also accounts of earnings (VII, Appendices I and II).

Elliot, A. R. D. 'Reviews and Magazines in the Early Years of the Nineteenth Century', *Cambridge History of English Literature*, XII, Cambridge, 1916, 140–63.

'The Emoluments of Publishing', *Publisher and Bookseller*, 27 May 1905, p. 219.

'The English Society', *Bulletin of the Authors' League of America*, II (May 1914), 8–13. On Society of Authors.

An Essay on the Antiquity, Dignity, and Advantages of Living in a Garret, London, 1751. One can see the bailiff from a greater distance.

Faber, Geoffrey. *A Publisher Speaking*, London, 1934. Discussion of agency, pp. 124–5.

——. 'Sailing Through the Air', *London Mercury*, XXXI (March 1935), 431–9. Reply to Herbert Read; see below.

Farrar, Larston D. *Successful Writers, and How They Work*, New York, 1959. Chapter on agency.

Fielding, Henry. *The Author's Farce*, London, 1730. On hack writers.

——. *The Covent Garden Journal*, London, 1752. Miscellaneous comments on authorship.

Findlater, Richard. *The Book Writers: Who Are They?*, London, 1966. Pamphlet.

——. *What Are Writers Worth?*, London, 1963. Pamphlet; a preliminary study for *The Book Writers*.

Flower, Sir Newman. *Just As It Happened*, New York, 1950. Memoirs; some material on the Pinkers.

Foote, Samuel. *The Author, a Comedy in Two Acts*, London, 1757. Love in a garret.

——. *The Patron, a Comedy in Three Acts*. London, 1764. Satirizes patrons and booksellers.

Ford, Ford Madox. *Return to Yesterday*, London, 1931. Pp. 58–64 on Pinker and Watt.

French, J. Milton. 'George Wither in Prison', *PMLA*, XLV (December 1930), 959–66.

Friederichs, Hulda. *The Life of Sir George Newnes*, London, 1911.

Furman, G., et al. *Memorial of G. Furman and Other Public Writers, Praying the Passage of an International Law of Copyright*, 20 February 1837. Unseen.

Furnivall, F. J. 'Pynson's Contracts with Horman for His *Vulgaria*, and Palsgrave for His *Lesclaircissement*, with Pynson's Letter of Denization', *Transactions of the Philological Society*, London, 1867, pp. 362–74. On costs of printing in 1545.

Fyfe, Hamilton. *Sixty Years of Fleet Street*, London, 1949. Material on the new reading public.

Gibbs, Sir Philip. *Adventures in Journalism*, New York and London, 1923. Memoirs.

Gibson, John. *Reminiscences of Sir Walter Scott*, Edinburgh, 1871. G. was Scott's law agent.

Gilfillan's Literary Portraits, ed. W. Robertson Nicoll, London, n.d. Includes memoir of G. by Nicoll.

Gill, Robert. *The Author, Publisher, Printer Complex*, Baltimore, 1940. An invitation to vanity publishing.

Gissing, George. *New Grub Street*, London, 1891.

Glen, James. 'Sir Walter Scott's Financial Transactions', in *The Letters of Sir Walter Scott*, ed. H. J. C. Grierson, I, 1787–1807, London, 1932, lxxx–xcv.

Goldring, Douglas. *The Last Pre-Raphaelite*, London, 1948. References to J. B. Pinker.

——. *South Lodge*, London, 1943. References to Pinker.

Goldsmith, Oliver. *The Citizen of the World*, in *Collected Works*, II, ed. Arthur Friedman, Oxford, 1966. See especially letters xxix–xxx (on authors' club), li (on bookseller), lvii and lxxxiv (on authors).

Goldsmith, Oliver. *An Enquiry into the Present State of Polite Learning in Europe*, London, 1774. Chapter X: 'Of Rewarding Genius in England.'
——. See under John Triplet.
Good, Alexander. *Why Your Manuscripts Return*, London, [1907]. How to write stories that sell, along with advice not to write poetry.
Gosse, Edmund. See *The Author* (London).
'The Great Unpublished Grows', *Guardian*, 17 January 1966. On amateur authors.
Greg, W. W. *English Literary Autographs, 1550–1625*, Oxford, 1925–32. Many of the autographs concern authors' finances.
——. *Some Aspects and Problems of London Publishing between 1550 and 1651*, Oxford, 1956.
Grierson, H. J. C. *Sir Walter Scott, Bart*, London, 1938.
The Grievances Between Authors and Publishers, London, 1887. Discussions by Walter Besant, Edmund Gosse, Frederick Pollock, Andrew Tuer, and others.
The Grub Street Journal (London, 1730+). Lead essays and communications often concern authors and booksellers.
Guide for the Writing Desk; or, Young Author's and Secretary's Friend, London, [1846?].
Guild of Literature and Art, [1854?]. Pamphlet describing bye-laws, activities and finances of the Guild.
Guild of Literature and Art. Prospectus of a New Endowment, in connection with an Insurance Company, for the Benefit of Men of Letters and Artists, London, [1851].
Gurko, Leo. *Giant In Exile*, New York, 1962. On Conrad; references to J. B. Pinker.
[H., T.] *The Author's Advocate and Young Publisher's Friend: A Sequel to the Perils of Authorship*, London, [c. 1840]. A few cynical and unreliable pages on the horrors of authorship and related matters.
——. *The Perils of Authorship . . . Containing Copious Instructions for Publishing Books at the Slightest Possible Risk*, London, [c. 1835]. 4th ed. c. 1840. Similar material to the preceding item. The author claims to have published 37 successful and 2 unsuccessful books.
Hackney, Alan. *Let's Keep Religion Out Of This!*, London, 1963. A novel in which the hero works for a literary agent.
Hackney, Iscariot. See Richard Savage.
Halsey, Francis Whiting. *Our Literary Deluge*, New York, 1902. Chapters III and IV on authors' finances.
[Hamilton, Arthur] *The Confessions of a Scribbler*, Merthyr Tydfil, [1879]. True story of an amateur author in the clutches of a vanity publisher.
Hammerton, J. A. *Barrie, the Story of a Genius*, London, 1929. References to A. A. Bright.
A Handbook for Writers and Artists, London, 1898. On markets.

The Hardships of Publishing. See William Heinemann.

Harvey, Jane. *Memoirs of an Author*, London, 1812. Unseen.

Hayes, Daniel. 'The Authors', in *Works In Verse*, London, 1769. Against literary hacks.

[Heinemann, William, ed.] *The Hardships of Publishing. Letters to 'The Athenaeum'*, London, 1893.

Heinemann, William. 'Publishing Simplified', *Publishers' Circular*, 30 November 1918, p. 456. Responses in succeeding issues up to 18 January 1919. Further comment by H. 6 December 1919, p. 525.

——. See also *The Academy, The Athenaeum, The Author* (London).

Hints and Directions for Authors in Writing, Printing and Publishing Their Works, London, 1842. From a vanity publisher, Edward Bull, and perhaps prepared by Bull himself.

'Historical Chronicle', *Gentleman's Magazine*, VI (June 1736), 353. First item concerns Society for the Encouragement of Learning.

Hitchcock, Frederick H. *The Building of a Book*, New York, 1929. Includes a chapter on agency.

Holbrook, David. 'Portrait of the Author as a Poor Man', *Guardian*, 4 November 1967, p. 6.

Hollister, Paul Merrick, ed. *The Author's Wallet*, New York, 1934. On price-fixing of books in eighteenth and nineteenth centuries.

Holt, Henry. 'The Commercialization of Literature', *Atlantic Monthly*, XCVI (November 1905), 576–600.

——. *Garrulities of an Octogenarian Editor*, Boston and New York, 1923. Pp. 206–13 on agency.

[Horne, Richard Henry] *Exposition of the False Medium and Barriers Excluding Men of Genius from the Public*, London, 1833.

——. 'Spirit of Modern Publishers', *Monthly Repository*, n.s., X (May 1836), 271–6. Contradicts opinion attacking publishers in *Exposition*.

Housman, Laurence. See *The Author* (London).

[Howells, William Dean] 'Editor's Study', *Harper's Magazine*, LXXX (March 1890), 642–7. On literature and money.

——. 'The Man of Letters as a Man of Business', *Harper's Magazine*, c. 1893. Unseen.

——. 'A Painful Subject', *Harper's Weekly*, XLVIII (9 January 1904), 48. On author–publisher.

How to Print and Publish a Book, Winchester, 1890. Unseen.

How to Publish; or, The Author's Handbook, London, [1908]. A brief guide through technical problems. Material on agency.

How to Publish, a Manual for Authors, London, 1857. From a vanity publisher, Partridge.

Hunt, Violet. *I Have This To Say* [*The Flurried Years*], New York, 1926. Comments on J. B. Pinker.

International Copyright. Meeting of Authors and Publishers, at the Rooms of the New York Historical Society, New York, 1868. Reprints speeches by both.

Jacobi, Charles Thomas. *On the Making and Issuing of Books*, London, 1891. A guide for authors. Revised edition, 1892, entitled *Some Notes on Books and Printing, a Guide for Authors, Publishers, & Others.*

Jay, Harriett. *Robert Buchanan*, London, 1903. Pp. 93–5 on B.'s unhappy dealings with an editor, 291 ff. on B. as his own publisher. B. apparently wrote a piece entitled 'Is Barabbas a Necessity?', *c.* 1896.

Jean-Aubry, G. *Joseph Conrad, Life and Letters*, 2 vols., New York, 1927. Letters to J. B. Pinker.

——. *The Sea Dreamer*, London, 1957. Material on Pinker.

Jerdan, William. *Autobiography*, 4 vols., London, 1852–3. III, Chapters X and XI, on Royal Society of Literature; IV, Chapters II and III, on miseries of authors.

——. *Illustrations of the Plan of a National Association for the Encouragement and Protection of Authors, and Men of Talent and Genius*, London, 1838. Discusses earlier societies, including Society for the Encouragement of Learning, 1735.

Jessop, Augustus. 'A Plea for the Publisher', *Contemporary Review*, LVII (March 1890), 380–6.

Johnson, Edgar. *Charles Dickens*, 2 vols., New York, 1952.

Johnson, Pamela Hansford. *Cork Street, Next to the Hatters*, London, 1965. Chapter 21 has unpleasant portrait of an agent.

Jonson, Ben. *Timber, or Discoveries*, in *Ben Jonson*, VIII, ed. C. H. Herford, Percy and Evelyn Simpson, Oxford, 1947. Comments on the profession of author.

Joseph, Michael. *Complete Writing for Profit*, London, [1930]. Includes Joseph's *The Commercial Side of Literature*, 1925. Pp. 464–83, 494–514 on agents.

Jovanovich, William. *Now, Barabbas*, New York and London, [1964]. Reflections of a commercial publisher.

[Judd, James, and Glass, Alexander Henry] *Counsels to Authors. Plans of Publishing, and Specimens of Types*, London, 1883. From a seemingly respectable publisher on commission, William Freeman.

Judge, Cyril Bathurst. *Elizabethan Book-Pirates*, Cambridge, Mass., 1934.

Kent, Elizabeth Eaton. *Goldsmith and His Booksellers*, Ithaca, New York, 1933.

Kirk, Eleanor. *Periodicals That Pay Contributors*, New York, 1890. Pamphlet, 1st ed. 1888.

Kirschbaum, Leo. *Shakespeare and the Stationers*, Columbus, Ohio, 1955.

Korg, Jacob. *George Gissing*, Seattle, Washington, 1963. Chapter VI on Gissing on Grub Street.

Lamb, Joseph B. *Practical Hints on Writing for the Press*, London, 1897. 'Published for the author'.

Lang, Andrew. 'At the Sign of the Ship', *Longman's Magazine*, XXIII (December 1893), 210–20. In defence of publishers.
——. 'Authors and Publishers', *Illustrated London News*, CI (24 December 1894), 814.
——. 'The Duties of Authors', *Illustrated London News*, CIV (17 March 1894), 327. Amateur authors plaguing Lang.
——. 'Literature as a Trade', *St. James's Gazette*, XXI (22 October 1890), 5.
——. 'The Wrongs of Authors', *Illustrated London News*, CVI (30 March 1895), 379.
Laski, Marghanita. 'The Reader Who Matters', *Guardian*, 25 August 1965, p. 6. On amateur authors plaguing established writers.
Lawrence, D. H. *Collected Letters*, 2 vols., ed. Harry T. Moore, New York, 1962. Material on J. B. Pinker, Curtis Brown.
'The League's Standard Agency Contract', *Bulletin of the Authors' League of America*, VII (August 1919), 15.
Leasor, James. *Author by Profession*, London, 1952. Sketches of several contemporary writers, with an introductory chapter on Grub Street.
A Letter from a Gentleman in Edinburgh, to His Friend in London: Concerning Literary Property, 1769.
A Letter to the Society of Booksellers, on the Method of Forming a True Judgment of the Manuscripts of Authors, London, 1738.
Lewis, Sinclair. *From Main Street to Stockholm*, ed. Harrison Smith, New York, 1952. Mainly letters between L. and his publisher.
'The Literary Agent', *Publisher and Bookseller*, 29 July 1905, p. 409.
'Literary Agents Who Poach', *Publishers' Circular*, 20 March 1920, pp. 319–20.
'The Literary Agent—Yes or No', *Bulletin of the Authors' League of America*, VII (June 1919), 7.
Literary Aspirant Magazine (London, 1846–7).
Literary Gazette (London), 7 September 1833, pp. 563–5; 14 September, pp. 580–2; 21 September, pp. 596–8. A three-part review-article on R. H. Horne, *Exposition*: see above.
Literary Mart (London, 1874–6). Includes complaints by authors against publishers.
Literary Year-Book (London, 1897+). Information every year on agency. After 1924 continued in part by *What Editors and Publishers Want* (Liverpool) until 1928.
Lord, William Jackson. *How Authors Make a Living: an Analysis of Free-Lance Writers' Incomes, 1953–1957*, University of Illinois (dissertation), 1961. Statistical study of some members of the Authors' League.
Lorimer, Adam [William Lorimer Watson]. *The Author's Progress*, Edinburgh and London, 1906. Informal discussion of the problems facing the young author. Includes discussion of publishers and Society of Authors.

Lowe, James. 'Gossip about Books and the Book World', *Everybody's Journal*, 29 October 1859, p. 76. On vanity publishers. Response in *Publishers' Circular*, 15 November 1859.

Lowndes, Marie Belloc. See *The Author* (London).

Lynch, Harriet. 'Authors' Adventures as Publishers. 1', *Bulletin of the Authors' League of America*, XII (November 1924), 11–12.

Lyon, Peter. *Success Story, the Life and Times of S. S. McClure*, New York, 1963.

M., J. *Reasons Humbly Offered for the Liberty of Unlicensed Printing*, London, 1693.

Macaulay, Catherine. *A Modest Plea for the Property of Copyright*, London, 1774.

McClure, S. S. *My Autobiography*, New York, 1914.

MacDonald, Greville. *George MacDonald and His Wife*, London, 1924. Material on A. P. Watt.

Mackail, Denis. *The Story of J. M. Barrie*, London, 1941. References to A. A. Bright.

McKay, George L. *Some Notes on Robert Louis Stevenson, His Finances and His Agents and Publishers*, New Haven, 1958.

McKerrow, Ronald B. 'Booksellers, Printers, and the Stationers' Trade', in *Shakespeare's England*, II, Oxford, 1916, 212–39.

[McKerrow, Ronald B.] 'Richard Robinson's *Eupolemia, Archippus* and *Panoplia* (1603)', *Gentleman's Magazine*, CCC (April 1906), 277–84.

Macmillan, Sir Frederick. *The Net Book Agreement 1899*, Glasgow, 1924. An account of the N.B. Agreement and *The Times* Book Club War.

'The Makers, Sellers and Buyers of Books', *Fraser's Magazine*, XLV (June 1852), 711–24. Reprinted by John W. Parker, London, 1852. Parker also issued *The Opinions of Certain Authors* (see below) on the same subject.

Marbury, Elisabeth. *My Crystal Ball*, New York, 1923. Memoirs.

A Memorial for the Booksellers of Edinburgh, [1743?]. Unseen.

Miller, Edwin Haviland. *The Professional Writer in Elizabethan England*, Cambridge, Mass., 1959.

Miller, Karl. 'Writers', *New Statesman*, LXXII (21 October 1966), 597. On a literary festival. Response 11 November, p. 700.

Miss Mallows Among the Publishers: a Sad Literary Experience. By Miss Mallows' Friend, Boston, 1881. A little book composed mainly of rejection slips.

Mitchell, Edwin Valentine. *The Art of Authorship*, New York, 1935. Chapter One on Grub Street. Negligible.

Moore, Thomas, et al. *Petition of Thomas Moore, and Other Authors of Great Britain, Praying Congress to Grant to Them the Exclusive Benefit of Their Writings within the United States*, 2 February 1837. Unseen.

More Reasons Humbly Offered to the House of Commons for the Bill to Encourage Learning and for Securing Property, [1709?]. Unseen.

Morgan, Charles. *The House of Macmillan*, London, 1943.

Morton, Charles W. *Frankly, George: or Letters to a Publisher from an Author Whose First Book is about to Appear*, Philadelphia and New York, 1951. Humorous presumption by the author; slight.

Mumby, Frank Arthur. *Publishing and Bookselling*, London, 1954. 1st ed. 1930.

My First Book, Intro. Jerome K. Jerome, London, 1894. Experiences of several popular authors, with occasional comments on finances.

Nash, Eveleigh. *I Liked the Life I Lived*, London, 1941. Memoirs.

Nashe, Thomas. *Works*, 5 vols., ed. Ronald B. McKerrow, Oxford, 1958. See especially I, *Pierce Penniless*, 149ff., and V, 16ff., on Nashe's finances.

Neill & Company's Guide to Authors in Correcting the Press, Edinburgh, [*c*. 1870]. A brief correction guide followed by specimens of type.

Neill & Company's Typographic Guide . . . for Authors and Publishers, Edinburgh, [*c*. 1880]. Same as preceding item but more elaborate.

Newman, Edward. *The Author's Guide for Printing*, London, [1875]. Nothing more than a small memorandum book for authors and scholars.

Newspaper Press Directory (London, 1846+).

Nicoll, W. Robertson. 'A. P. Watt, the Great Napoleon of the Realm of Print', *British Weekly*, LVII (12 November 1914), 127.

——. 'Authors and Publishers', *Bookman* (New York), I (July 1895), 390–2.

——. 'The Literary Agent', *Bookman* (New York), I (May 1895), 249–51.

Nichols, John. *Literary Anecdotes of the Eighteenth Century*, 9 vols., London, 1812–16. Sketches of many booksellers. VIII, 293ff., lists payments to authors by Bernard and Henry Lintot.

Nisbet, Hume. *The Author, the 'Ghost', and the Society*, London, 1904. Attack on Society of Authors.

Nutt, Alfred. See *The Academy*.

O. and Y. *The Author As Publisher: or Why Don't Authors Publish Their Own Books*, London, 1912. Authors can't possibly do a worse job for themselves than the publishers are doing.

O'Brien, M. B. *A Manual for Authors, Printers, and Publishers*, London, 1890. Unseen.

The Opinions of Certain Authors on the Bookselling Question, London, 1852. Concerns the underselling of books; letters from Carlyle, Darwin, and many others to the publisher John Parker. See also above *Additional Letters*, John Chapman, and 'The Makers, Sellers, and Buyers of Books'.

Orcutt, William Dana. *The Author's Desk Book*, New York, 1914. Material on agency, pp. 63–4.

Oxford Author's Style Book, New York, 1943. For the house author.

[Page, Walter Hines] *A Publisher's Confession*, London, 1905. On the hardships of publishing. Originally appeared as articles in the *Boston Evening Transcript*.

Page, Walter Hines. See *The Writer* (Boston).

Palmer, Herbert E. *What the Public Wants*, London, n.d. A satirical pamphlet on a writer who can't please editors.

'The Panel Game', *Times Literary Supplement*, 20 October 1966, p. 959. On Arts Council grants to authors. Correspondence on subject throughout rest of year.

Parker, Wyman W. *Henry Stevens of Vermont*, Amsterdam, 1963.

Paston, George. *At John Murray's, Records of a Literary Circle*, London, 1932.

Paterson, T. V. *How to Get Money Quickly; or, Thirty Ways of Making a Fortune*, London, [1868?]. Endpapers concern agency.

Perkins, Maxwell Evarts. *Editor to Author, the Letters of Maxwell E. Perkins*, ed. John Hall Wheelock, New York and London, 1950. To Thomas Wolfe, Ernest Hemingway, and others.

Petheram, John. *Reasons for Establishing an Authors' Publication Society*, London, 1843.

The Petition of the Booksellers of London, 1735. Unseen.

Philips, John. *The Splendid Shilling*, London, 1705. Mock heroic poem on authorship. See next item.

Philips, Katherine. *The Crooked Sixpence, with a Learned Preface*, London, 1743. Preface argues that *The Splendid Shilling* was the work of a dishonest publisher and his hacks, based on Katherine Philips's earlier poem (*c.* 1667) and falsely attributed to John Philips.

Phillips, J. S. R. 'The Growth of Journalism', *Cambridge History of English Literature*, XIV, Cambridge, 1917, 167–204.

Plant, Marjorie. *The English Book Trade*, London, 1939.

Pocket Printing Guide. Unseen. Predecessor of *Comprehensive Guide*; see above.

The Poet's Magazine (London, 1859–60). Unseen.

The Poet's Magazine (London, 1876+; later title *Authors and Artists*; other titles). Unseen.

Pollard, Alfred W. *Shakespeare Folios and Quartos*, London, 1909. Chapter I on publishing in Shakespeare's day.

——. *Shakespeare's Fight with the Pirates and the Problems of the Transmission of His Text*, London, 1917.

Pollard, Graham. 'Serial Fiction', in *New Paths in Book Collecting*, ed. John Carter, London, 1934.

Pollock, Sir Frederick. 'Some Considerations on Publishing', *Pall Mall Gazette*, LVI (1 May 1893), 3.

——. See also *The Grievances Between Authors*.

Pond, J. B. *Eccentricities of Genius*, New York, 1900. Memoirs.

Pope, Alexander. *The Dunciad*, London, 1728.

Pote, Joseph. *A Letter to A . . . B . . . Esq: Concerning Subscriptions*, London, 1737.

——. *A Second Letter Concerning the Compleat Edition of Dr. Cave's Historia Literaria*, London, 1739. Same subject as preceding item.

Pound, Reginald. *Arnold Bennett*, New York, 1953. Material on the Pinkers.

The Prentice-Hall Author's Manual, New York, 1937. For the house author.

Price, Warren. *The Literature of Journalism*, Minneapolis, Minnesota, 1959. A bibliography.

Pritchard, Allan. 'George Wither's Quarrel with the Stationers', *Studies in Bibliography*, XVI (1963), 27–42.

Prospectus of a New Periodical Work, to be called 'The Author's Review, and Literary Protector', London, 1812. Uncertain whether the journal was ever published. The Prospectus attacks anonymous reviewing and offers the new journal as a forum for authors to reply to unjust criticism.

'Public Patronage of Men of Letters', *Fraser's Magazine*, XXXIII (January 1846), 58–71.

'Publishers', *Pall Mall Gazette*, 2 July 1866, p. 10. On good and bad ones.

Publisher and Bookseller (London, 1905–7). A few items listed separately.

'Publishers and Authors', *Fraser's Magazine*, XXXVIII (October 1848), 411–20.

The Publishers' Circular (London, 1837+). Useful information week by week on author–publisher. A few items listed separately.

Purdy, Richard. *Thomas Hardy, a Bibliographical Study*, London, 1954. Appendix III on Tillotson Syndicate.

Putnam, George Haven. *Authors and Publishers*, New York, 1883. 7th ed. 1897. Chapter on agency in 7th ed.

——. 'Authors' Complaints and Publishers' Profits', *Forum*, XII (September 1891), 62–77.

——. *George Palmer Putnam*, New York and London, 1912.

Quarterly Review, VIII (September 1812), 93–114. Unfavourable review-article on D'Israeli's *Calamities of Authors*.

The Question Concerning Literary Property, Determined by the Court of King's Bench on 20th April, 1769, in the Case between Andrew Millar and Robert Taylor, London, 1773.

[Ralph, James] *The Case of Authors by Profession or Trade, Stated. With Regard to Booksellers, the Stage, and the Public. No Matter by Whom*, London, 1758.

Read, Herbert. 'The Sweated Author', *London Mercury*, XXXI (February 1935), 333–40. See Geoffrey Faber for reply.

Reed, Alexander Wyclif. *The Author-Publisher Relationship*, Wellington, New Zealand, 1946. Unseen.

Reeve, James Knapp. *Practical Authorship*, Ridgewood, New Jersey, [*c*. 1917]. 1st ed. *c*. 1899. For amateur authors.

Reynolds, Paul R., Jr. *The Writer and His Markets*, New York, 1959.

——. *The Writing Trade*, Boston, 1949. Pp. 96–108 on agency.

[Richardson, Samuel] *The Case of Samuel Richardson, of London, Printer, With Regard to the Invasion of His Property*, London, 1753. Pirating of *Sir Charles Grandison*.

Rickword, Edgell. 'The Social Setting', in *Guide to English Literature*, v, ed. Boris Ford, London, 1962, 11–30.

Robbins, J. Albert. 'Fees Paid to Authors by Certain American Periodicals, 1840–1850', *Studies in Bibliography*, II (1949–50), 95–104.

Roberts, D. Kilham. Articles on agency in *The Authors' Handbook* and *The Book World*, which see.

Roberts, W. *The Elizabethan Grub Street*, London, 1891. Reprinted from *The Antiquary*, August 1891. A brief account.

Robinson, Sir John. 'Charles Dickens and the Guild of Literature and Art', *Cornhill Magazine*, xvi (January 1904), 28–33.

Robinson, Kenneth. *Wilkie Collins*, London, 1951. References to A. P. Watt.

Rolfe, Frederick William [Baron Corvo]. *Letters to Grant Richards*, Hurst, Berkshire, 1952. Author to publisher, 1899–1902.

Rosenberg, Eleanor. *Leicester, Patron of Letters*, New York, 1955.

Rossetti, Dante Gabriel. *The Letters of Dante Gabriel Rossetti to His Publisher, F. S. Ellis*, ed. Oswald Doughty, London, 1928.

Ruskin, John. *Works*, 39 vols., London, 1903–12. Vols. 27–29, *Fors Clavigera*, letters 6, 11, 16, 57, concern his publishing.

Russell, Percy. *The Authors' Manual*, London, [*c*. 1894]. 7th ed.; 1st ed. 1890. Broad discussion of literary types; some practical advice on commercial writing.

——. *The Literary Manual, or, A Complete Guide to Authorship*, London, 1886. More concerned with journalism than *The Authors' Manual*.

Sadleir, Michael. *Authors and Publishers. A Study in Mutual Esteem*, London and Toronto, 1932. Slight.

Saintsbury, George. 'Milton', *Cambridge History of English Literature*, vii, Cambridge, 1911, 95–138.

[Saunders, Frederic] *The Author's Printing and Publishing Assistant*, New York, 1839. Also London, 1842 (4th ed.). Issued by Saunders, New York, and Saunders and Otley, London. Aimed in part at authors who will publish on commission.

Savage, Raymond. See *The Author* (London).

[Savage, Richard] *An Author to be Let*, London, *c*. 1730. Pamphlet in which Iscariot Hackney offers his services.

——. *Works . . .*, *with an Account of the Life and Writings of the Author by Samuel Johnson*, 2 vols., London, 1765. The life has much on S.'s writing conditions.

[Sawyer, Charles James] *Dickens v. Barabbas*, London, 1930.

Scholes, Robert. 'Grant Richards to James Joyce', *Studies in Bibliography*, XVI (1963), 139–60. Mainly concerns publishing of *Dubliners*.

Scintilla, or A Light Broken Into Dark Warehouses, with Observations upon the Monopolists of Seven Several Patents and Two Charters, Practiced and Performed by a Mystery of Some Printers, Sleeping Stationers, and Combining Booksellers, 1641. Pamphlet on dishonest means by which printers increase their profits.

The Search for a Publisher, London, 1855. 8th ed. 1881. Issued by a succession of vanity publishers.

'The Secret Agents', *Observer*, 29 November 1964.

Shand, Alexander Innes. 'The Novelists and Their Patrons', *Fortnightly Review*, XLVI (July 1886), 23–35.

Shaw, George Bernard. See *The Author* (London).

Sheavyn, Phoebe. *The Literary Profession in the Elizabethan Age*, Manchester, 1909. Revised edition, 1968.

Sheehan, Donald. *This Was Publishing*, Bloomington, Indiana, 1952. American publishing in the gilded age; material on agents.

Shepherd, William. *Authors and Authorship*, New York, 1882. Miscellaneous discussion of the situation of the author.

Sherard, Robert H. 'Authors Their Own Publishers', *Westminster Gazette*, 14 October 1895, pp. 1–2. Account of a recent French organization. Correspondence 21 October, p. 3; 22 October, p. 3; 23 October, p. 2.

Sinclair, May. See *The Author* (London).

Sinclair, Upton. 'Authors' Adventures as Publishers. 2', *Bulletin of the Authors' League of America*, XII (February 1925), 7–9.

Singleton, Frank. *Tillotsons, 1850–1950*, Bolton and London, 1950.

Smiles, Samuel. 'Authors and Publishers', *Murray's Magazine*, VII (January 1890), 48–61; (February) 207–19.

——. *A Publisher and His Friends, Memoir and Correspondence of the late John Murray*, London, 1891.

Smith, D. Nichol. 'Authors and Patrons', in *Shakespeare's England*, II, Oxford, 1916, 182–211.

Smith, Russell Edgar. 'The Value of an Author's Agent', *Magazine Maker* (also called *Writer's Bulletin and Literary Reporter*), III (October 1912), 10–12. Slight.

Some Thoughts on the Present State of Printing and Bookselling, London, 1709. Unseen.

[Southward, John] *Authorship and Publication. A Guide to Matters Relating to Printing and Publishing*, London, 1882. Unseen.

Spedding, James. *Publishers and Authors*, London, 1867.

Spon, Ernest. *How to Publish a Book*, London, 1872. Spon was the publisher as well. To judge from the book, he must have been the most reputable sort of vanity publisher.

Sprigge, S. Squire. *The Methods of Publishing*, London, 1890. Advice to authors from the Society of Authors.

——. *The Society of French Authors*, London, n.d.

Stackhouse, Thomas. *The Bookbinder, Bookprinter, and Bookseller Confuted: or, The Author's Vindication of Himself*, London, 1732. S.'s difficulties with the bookbinder, etc.

Stower, C[aleb]. *The Printer's Price-Book*, London, 1814. Some advice to authors included.

——. *Typographical Marks Employed in Correcting Proofs, Explained and Exemplified; For the Use of Authors*, London, 1806. 2nd ed.

Super, R. H. *The Publication of Landor's Works*, London, Bibliographical Society, 1954. Supplement to the Bibliographical Society's Transactions No. 18. On Landor's relations with publishers.

Sutherland, James. *Defoe*, London, 1937. See especially Chapter v, on Defoe's paid political writing.

Swinnerton, Frank. *Authors and the Book Trade*, London, 1932. Chapter on agency.

——. *Background With Chorus*, London, 1956. On J. B. Pinker, pp. 128–129, 215.

——. *The Bookman's London*, London, 1951. Remarks on agency, pp. 56–57.

——. *Swinnerton, an Autobiography*, New York, 1936. Material on Pinker.

Thackeray, William Makepeace. *The History of Pendennis*, 2 vols., London, 1849–50. Chapters 31ff. touch on Grub Street.

Thirkell, Angela. *Pomfret Towers*, London, 1938. Allusions to agents, p. 238 and elsewhere.

Thomas, Moy. Untitled article, *Publishers' Circular*, XXXVIII (16 March 1875), 193–6. On Association to Protect the Rights of Authors (see above), of which Thomas was Secretary.

Thomson, Christine Campbell. *I Am a Literary Agent*, London, 1951. Memoirs.

Thring, G. Herbert. 'The Literary Agent', in *Who's Who among Authors and Writers*, London, 1934–5, p. 835.

——. See *The Author* (London).

The Times. Accounts of discussions sponsored by Society of Authors on the grievances of authors, and responses by publishers: 3 March 1887, p. 6; 10 March, p. 8; 11 March, p. 10; 12 March, p. 6; 14 March, p. 6; 24 March, p. 13; 28 March, p. 3.

'To the Author of The Weekly Journal', *The Weekly Journal or Saturday's Post*, 20 March 1725, pp. 2075–6. Attacks the indifference of bookseller-publishers to the needs of the public; incidental comment on the hardships of authors.

Tobin, John. *The School for Authors*, London, 1808. A farce involving an author and a critic as suitors of the same woman.

Todd, Charles Burr. 'The Case of the American Author', *Forum*, XIII (March 1892), 107–14.

——. 'The Forerunner of the Authors' League—The American Authors' Guild', *Bulletin of the Authors' League of America*, VI (September 1918), 6–8.

'Towards Processed Literature', *Times Literary Supplement*, 27 May 1965, pp. 406–7. On the modern editor as literary friend and adviser.

'The Trade of Literature', *Gentleman's Magazine*, CCCII (January 1907), 1–4.

Train, Arthur. *Apologia Pro Officio Suo*, Privately printed [*c*. 1928]. On the Authors' League.

Transactions of the Royal Society of Literature (London). Vol. I, 1829, contains the Charter and Bye-laws of the Royal Society.

Triplet, John [poss. pseud. of Oliver Goldsmith]. 'Distresses of a Hired Writer', *British Magazine*, II (April 1761), 198–200.

Trollope, Anthony. *An Autobiography*, New York, 1883.

——. *Letters*, ed. Bradford Booth, London and New York, 1951.

——. 'On the Best Means of Extending and Securing an International Law of Copyright', *Transactions of the National Association for the Promotion of Social Science*, *c*. 1876. Unseen.

Tuer, Andrew. See *The Grievances Between Authors*.

Twain, Mark. *Mark Twain's Letters to His Publishers 1867–1894*, ed. Hamlin Hill, Berkeley and Los Angeles, 1967.

Unwin, Sir Stanley. *The Truth about Publishing*, London 1926. 4th ed. 1946, with additions; material on agency 74–9, 289–94, and elsewhere.

Uzzell, Thomas H. *Writing as a Career*, New York, 1938. Advice on markets by a well-known agent for amateur authors.

A Vindication of the Exclusive Right of Authors to Their Own Works: a Subject now under Consideration before the Twelve Judges of England, London, 1762.

Vogt, George McGill. 'Richard Robinson's *Eupolemia* (1603)', *Studies in Philology*, XXI (October 1924), 629–48. Mainly a transcription of the whole of *Eupolemia*.

W., F. 'An Interview with Mr. A. P. Watt', *Bookman* (London), III (October 1892), 20–2.

W., W. 'Why Virtue and Merit are Rarely Rewarded', *Fraser's Magazine*, LXI (April 1860), 474–85. On authors' complaints.

Wagner, Leopold. *How to Publish a Book or Article*, London, 1898. Comprehensive advice to literary aspirants; pp. 106–10 on agency.

Walpole, Hugh. See *The Author* (London).

[Warburton, William] *An Enquiry into the Nature and Origin of Literary Property*, London, 1762.

———. *A Letter from an Author, to a Member of Parliament, Concerning Literary Property*, London, 1747.

Warendrof, M. M. E. H. 'Literary Agents', *Publishers' Circular*, CXLV (19 September 1936), 422–4.

Watkins, Ann. *Literature For Sale*, New York, 1941. Pamphlet, recollections of an agent.

Watson, E. H. Lacon. *Hints to Young Authors*, London, 1902. On agency, pp. 134–44.

———. 'The Literary Agent in England', *Bulletin of the Authors' League of America*, I (January 1914), 11–13.

Watson, Elmo Scott. *A History of Newspaper Syndicates in the United States, 1865–1935*, Chicago, 1936.

Waugh, Alec. See *The Author* (London).

Waugh, Arthur. *A Hundred Years of Publishing*, London, 1930. On agents, pp. 203–7.

———. *One Man's Road*, London, 1931. On agents, pp. 230 and 306ff.

Webb, R. K. 'The Victorian Reading Public', *Guide to English Literature*, VI, ed. Boris Ford, London, 1963, 205–26.

Weber, Carl. *The Rise and Fall of James Ripley Osgood*, Waterville, Maine, 1959. An early publisher's agent in America.

Wells, H. G. *Mankind in the Making*, London, 1903. Pp. 375–90 propose government support of authors. And see *The Author* (London).

Welsh, Charles. *Publishing a Book*, Boston, 1899. Guide for authors.

What Editors and Publishers Want. See *Literary Year-Book*.

What Every Writer Should Know about Publishing His Own Book, New York, 1957. Pamphlet reprinting two articles by Edward Uhlan, head of Exposition Press, a vanity press, and an article on him.

Wheatley, Henry B. *The Dedication of Books to Patron and Friend*, London, 1887.

Whyte, Frederic. *William Heinemann*, London, 1928. On agents, pp. 122–128.

Wild, John A. *Cost of Production*, London, 1909. A guide for printers. See also above, *The Cost of Publishing* and Caleb Stower.

Williams, J. B. [Joseph George Muddiman]. 'The Beginnings of English Journalism', *Cambridge History of English Literature*, VII, Cambridge, 1911, 343–65.

Winter, John Strange [Mrs. Henrietta Eliza Vaughan Stannard]. *Confessions of a Publisher*, New York, 1892. Light tale of a vanity publisher whose son loves a lady writer.

Wither, George. *The Schollers Purgatory, Discovered in the Stationers Commonwealth*, London [c. 1624].

Wolcot, Dr. John (Peter Pindar). *Works*, 5 vols., London, 1812. See I, 'A Poetical, Supplicating, Modest, and Affecting Epistle to Those Literary Colossuses, the Reviewers.'

Woodberry, George E. 'Literature in the Market-Place', *Forum*, XI (August 1891), 652–61.

Wright, Louis B. *Middle-Class Culture in Elizabethan England*, Chapel Hill, North Carolina, 1935. See especially Chapter IV on popular literary taste and the writer's situation.

The Writer (Boston, 1887+). A few items on author–publisher, mainly concerned with agents, on the following dates: June 1891 (on literary bureau); March 1900 (Walter Hines Page on author–publisher); September 1906; July 1908 (on author–publisher); October 1910 (William Heinemann on agents); February 1917; June 1918; November 1918; March 1919; April 1926; October 1926; March 1927; October 1929; February 1933; March–April 1934; April 1935; November 1936; June 1940; August 1940; September 1940; July 1967.

The Writer (London, 1888–9). Unseen.

The Writer and Reader (London, 1888). Designed to counteract bad reviewing, it gave space to authors to provide objective descriptions of their published works.

The Writer and the Publisher, University of Missouri Bulletin, XXV (1924), Journalism Series No. 29. Misleading title; inconsequential pieces on various aspects of newspaper work.

The Writer's Handbook, ed. A. S. Burack, Boston, 1955. Includes material on agency, some or all of it from issues of *The Writer* (Boston).

The Writers' Year-Book (London, 1902+).

Yard, Robert Sterling. *The Publisher*, New York, 1913. Reflections of the editor of *Century Magazine*. Chapter IV: 'Publisher, Author, and the Devil.'

Young, Edward. *Two Epistles to Mr. Pope, Concerning the Authors of the Age*, London, 1730.

Young, John L. *Books: From the MS. to the Bookseller*, London, 1929. Material on author–publisher–agent.

The Young Poet's Assistant in Composition, London, 1854. Unseen.

INDEX